"This is such an important book! Patrick M. Duffy has translated research and clinical knowledge into workable steps to help parents turn behavior around at home before turning to professionals for help. This book empowers parents to have confidence in themselves and gives them the knowledge and tools to help their children by focusing on reestablishing a good parent/child relationship. The examples throughout the book will help parents recognize they are not alone in dealing with these problems. Every family service, school advisor, and family doctor should have a copy of this book—and encourage parents to read it!"

—**Bernadette Christensen** is clinical director at The Norwegian Center for Child Behavioral Development and teaches in the psychology department at the University of Oslo, Norway

"How terrific that Patrick M. Duffy has made available to parents the practical and effective strategies that have been developed through almost twenty years of research. With this readable and immediately useful handbook, a parent of a youth who has persistent problems with self-regulation and non-compliance will be able to access intervention strategies utilized in approaches like multisystemic therapy—the most comprehensively researched, evidence-based intervention for teenagers whose behaviors lead them down a pathway into the juvenile justice system. Parents and behavioral health clinicians can take the pragmatic ideas and straightforward practices currently only accessible to a small number of families and put them immediately into practice. More importantly, they will likely see positive results in the behavior of their teenager! Yes, it requires a parent to alter his or her current parenting style—not an easy task—but the outcome in terms of youth success and family harmony are well worth the effort."

—**Eric W. Trupin, PhD,** professor and vice chairman at the University of Washington School of Medicine

"Patrick Duffy's book provides the kind of real-world guidance that is distinctly pragmatic and direct. While he clearly conveys empathy for parents of very troubled youth, he simultaneously reinforces the goal of striving for warmth and control as the critical element of the parent-child relationship. Duffy draws on both research and his considerable experience with this population of youth and their families. The breadth and diversity of the stories, strategies, and techniques contained in this volume should provide many parents with some of the tools they need to achieve a more positive relationship with their child, and find a sense of hope in sustaining it. While Duffy does not eschew professional guidance as needed, his focus is on helping parents gain confidence and skills in effectively managing their children's behavior. This is a significant resource for parents whose teens are on the edge of—or in—the red zone, and without effective intervention face terribly negative and cascading consequences."

—**Patrick J. Kanary,** director at the Center for Innovative Practices at the Institute for the Study and Prevention of Violence at Kent State University

# Parenting Your Delinquent, Defiant, or Out-of-Control Teen

## How to Help Your Teen Stay in School and Out of Trouble Using an Innovative Multisystemic Approach

### PATRICK M. DUFFY, JR., PSYD

New Harbinger Publications, Inc.

## Publisher's Note

*This publication is designed to provide accurate and authoritative information in regard to the subject matter covered. It is sold with the understanding that the publisher is not engaged in rendering psychological, financial, legal, or other professional services. If expert assistance or counseling is needed, the services of a competent professional should be sought.*

Distributed in Canada by Raincoast Books

Copyright © 2014 by Patrick M. Duffy, Jr.
New Harbinger Publications, Inc.
5674 Shattuck Avenue
Oakland, CA 94609
www.newharbinger.com

Cover design by Amy Shoup
Acquired by Melissa Kirk
Edited by Elizabeth Berg

### Library of Congress Cataloging-in-Publication Data

Duffy, Patrick M., Jr.
  Parenting your delinquent, defiant, or out-of-control teen : how to help your teen stay in school and out of trouble using an innovative multisystemic approach / Patrick M. Duffy, Jr.
      pages cm
  Includes bibliographical references.
    ISBN 978-1-62625-083-3 (paperback) -- ISBN 978-1-62625-084-0 (pdf e-book) -- ISBN 978-1-62625-085-7 (epub)  1.  Problem children. 2.  Parenting. 3.  Teenager and parent. I. Title.
  HQ773.D84 2014
  305.235--dc23

                                    2014033246

Printed in the United States of America

16      15      14

10      9      8      7      6      5      4      3      2      1                    First printing

To my wonderful parents, my loving wife, Kelly,
my precious girls, Regan and Ava, my sister and brother,
and the next generation of the Duffy family. May the
material of this book be irrelevant to you.

# Contents

# Acknowledgments

To acknowledge the people who were crucial to the completion of this work, I must begin with those who supported and encouraged me throughout the process. I first shared the idea with my parents, Katherine and Michael Duffy, and as usual, they were very supportive and encouraged me throughout the effort, only to be thanked by being tasked with initial editing.

My lovely wife, Kelly Duffy, has provided support, love, and encouragement as this project progressed. Without such a loving relationship, this text would still be incomplete. For her effort, she too was tasked with initial editing.

I can say with absolute certainty that this book would not have been written without my experiences with evidence-based approaches like multisytemic therapy (MST). The views presented in this book, however, are my own and do not necessarily reflect those of MST Services or the developers of the MST model.

I would like to thank my agent, Rita Rosenkranz, for giving me a chance. Without her support and guidance, this text would have remained confined to my hard drive.

Melissa Kirk, acquisitions editor for New Harbinger Publications, saw potential in this project, and she and Jess Beebe, editorial manager, provided invaluable support and suggestions. Elizabeth Berg, freelance editor, was instrumental in refining the text for clarity and brevity. Thanks to them and the entire team at New Harbinger Publications for bringing this to fruition.

# Introduction

If you have picked up this book, you are most likely frustrated with trying to manage your teenager's behavior. Although you may feel alone in your efforts, I can assure you that there are many families facing a similar struggle. The Office of Juvenile Justice and Delinquency Prevention (Snyder 2008, 1) reports that in 2006 alone, law enforcement officers made an estimated 2.2 million arrests of people under the age of eighteen. The report also shows that juveniles accounted for 17 percent of violent crimes and 26 percent of property crimes in 2006. And these numbers, while staggering, still do not account for youths who are getting into trouble but have not been arrested.

The data regarding juvenile substance abuse does little to ease concern. According to the National Institute on Drug Abuse (2008), 28.3 percent of kids between the ages of twelve and twenty reported drinking in the month prior to the survey, and 12.4 percent reported having driven under the influence within the previous year. The data does suggest a decline in marijuana use, but 24.6 percent of tenth graders reported use in the past year, as well as 31.7 percent of twelfth graders. The use of cocaine has remained stable among children twelve and older. More troubling findings are the decline in perceived harmfulness of hallucinogenic drugs and the increased abuse of prescription drugs.

Decades of research has been conducted on the causes and correlates of delinquency as well as on methods of addressing these behaviors. Blueprints for Violence Prevention, an independent research project of the Center for the Study and Prevention of Violence at the University of Colorado, has created stringent research and effectiveness criteria with which to evaluate the effectiveness of programs targeting youth violence. The researchers have evaluated more than nine hundred such programs and have identified twelve that they consider effective, or model, programs. They currently list nineteen additional programs that show promise (Blueprints for Violence Prevention 2006; 2009). These research-proven approaches can help families get their children's behavior under control. They have been shown to be effective, but they are not made available to the public on a large scale. Rather, they are practiced in areas where decision makers and funders have been willing to risk political capital and follow research data to disrupt the status quo. However, despite resistance from some in the service community and the justice community, use of these approaches is growing.

Given the relatively low availability of evidence-based programs, the vast majority of families, and possibly yourself, are forced to manage their children on their own without any guidance from research. Some naively enroll their children in expensive treatment regimens that have little chance of working. Even worse, some popular approaches have actually been shown to increase the likelihood of juveniles committing offenses.

It will probably come as no surprise that one of the biggest predictors of delinquent behavior is whether a child associates with other kids who commit delinquent acts (Dishion et al. 1996; Prinstein and Dodge 2008). Considering the effects of peer approval on delinquent behavior, it seems logical that Dishion, McCord, and Poulin (1999) found that intervention efforts with youths in groups not only failed to diminish delinquent behavior but made such behavior more likely. This is consistent with the finding of the Washington State

Institute for Public Policy (Aos, Miller, and Drake 2006) that programs like Scared Straight and boot camps increase the likelihood of violence.

The good news is that there are approaches that work, and this book is based on their common elements. Among the programs shown by research to be effective are those designed to work with the child in the community and through various influences on the child's behavior. The most effective "are multisystemic in nature," with programs such as multidimensional treatment foster care, functional family therapy (FFT), and multisystemic therapy (MST) among the most commonly cited (Sexton 2010; Aos, Miller, and Drake 2006; Blueprints for Violence Prevention 2009). These programs are all designed to work with the specific factors that research indicates are predictive of delinquent behavior.

Since I have revealed the truth about programs that are effective and those that are not, I would like to begin this book with a disclaimer. I have no research to suggest nor am I claiming that reading this book is equivalent to going through FFT, MST, or any other evidence-based practice with a qualified therapist from a licensed program. However, I can tell you with certainty that the information given in this book is the best available and is based on the same research regarding the causes of delinquency as the treatment programs proven to be the most effective. I am offering you the information that I have found to be the most important in my experience with evidence-based practices. Furthermore, if this book has no effect on your ability to improve your child's behavior, yet it convinces you not to send your child to a program that research shows will increase the likelihood of delinquency, then you and I have effectively reduced juvenile crime.

This book provides parents and families with some information on the factors that support or encourage a teen's difficult behavior and some strategies to address this behavior. I recommend that you read the entire book before implementing any of the strategies outlined. This work is doable, but it is not easy; if it was, you would never have needed this book. It is important that you understand the broad outlines of the necessary tasks before randomly trying strategies outlined in this book. Many books that offer a new discipline strategy fall short by failing to consider the broad range of influences on the child. As you will see, there is much more to the picture than you can address by just grounding your child.

Before we move forward, let me define the behaviors for which this book is appropriate. This book is for parents of children with significant behavior problems. The intensity of the strategies outlined may not be appropriate for a child who merely stomps his feet and mumbles about doing chores as he does them. It is also not about a child who keeps a messy room or does not want to be seen with her parents around friends. Before you tell me exactly how it is your child talks back to you, let me specify that I am referring to truancy, fighting, stealing, drug and alcohol use, and other illegal offenses, which go far beyond the realm of rudeness. The principles discussed in this book are certainly relevant to more benign, though irritating, behavior and can be applied to it, but the intensity of the effort differs. As is the case with each child and family, it must be tailored to fit the need.

In this book, you will learn about the various factors that years of research have shown to be connected to delinquent behavior. You will also learn about some common methods for targeting those factors and thus eliminating that which contributes to your child's troublesome behavior. I will share strategies that I have seen parents use with success during my years working with delinquent youths. (All identifying information in these examples has been changed, and any resemblance the stories may have to you or anyone you know is purely accidental.) To be successful, your efforts must be tailored to the specific influences present in your child's life. There is no one right answer for how to get children to stop using drugs, but there is one for how to stop *your* child from using. That answer will be different from what works for many other kids, but you need worry only about yours. This book will help you take an honest look at your child's life and environment and pinpoint key elements that could make a significant difference in her behavior. From this point, your willingness and determination will be deciding factors.

Throughout this book, you will be given examples of things that parents can or should do differently. You will also be given exercises to help move you along. I will address also some common concerns parents have when working with their child's troublesome behaviors. Hopefully, you are spending time with this book out of a real desire to make changes. It is crucial that you not think that I intend, or that this book intends, to blame parents for their child's behavior. If that were the case, you would rightly discard the book (I used a gentle term since it's my book) and move on to something else. Parents should realize that their children's behavior is determined by multiple influences present in the environment. I start with the parents because parents are closest to the child, and they have the most power and greatest motivation to create change. My goal is to teach parents to be effective in making that change happen.

What you are doing now as a parent may work with many other kids, but it has not been effective with your child; if it had, you would be in a different section of the bookstore. I say these things to let you know from the beginning that I do not blame you for your child's behavior. However, I see you as the person with the most power to change it. You will be confronted with some tasks that may seem difficult, and they will be, but be assured: change is possible.

# PART 1

# Why Is This Happening?

# Chapter 1

# Causes of Delinquency and Appropriate Action

In this book, "delinquent behavior," "troubling behavior," "problem behavior," and other such terms will be used in reference to serious behavior problems. Specifically, I am referring to behavior that would be considered intentional misbehavior, such as truancy, drug and alcohol use, vandalism, theft, violence, running away, and other actions of such significance as to make you consider sending your child to a treatment program. If your child's behavior is explained by a psychiatric or developmental challenge, another approach would be more appropriate. Beyond ruling out such a condition, this book is not about making a diagnosis. Different therapists would likely debate whether your child's behavior is oppositional defiant disorder or meets the standards of a conduct disorder or attention deficit/ hyperactivity disorder (ADHD). As the writer of this book, I do not care. You can call it what you want, but the fact is that Johnny is drinking and fighting and needs to stop. I am not going to discuss disorders, because the correct label does not really matter to me or to you, and it is not what will make a child stop drinking and fighting. Nor does that label satisfy the neighbors who just had their window busted. What would satisfy everyone, including the debating therapists, would be for Johnny to stop drinking and fighting. The goal of this book is to help you make that happen rather than to label the behavior; you already know what the problem is.

# Contributors to Delinquent Behavior

Now that we have identified the behavior, let's take a look at the factors that contribute to it. We can probably all agree that a child's behavior is influenced by other people. Decades of study have told us that a juvenile's behavior is determined by multiple influences from the environment, including the family, the peer group, the school, the neighborhood, and the broader community (Huizinga, Loeber, and Thornberry 1995).

## It's All Related

It is important to understand that all the areas listed above affect one another, and tend to work in predictable sequences or patterns. Just as a car has many parts, or systems, which must work well together, your child's environment is made up of many parts, or systems, that work to produce or allow a particular pattern of behavior. Each of these systems has an influence over your teen's behavior. They also influence each other.

For example, if a child exhibits threatening behavior toward a parent and is given what he wants as a result, he is likely to use the same behavior to get his way the next time. The parent has essentially rewarded him for the threatening behavior. In this way, the parent's behavior increases the child's threatening behavior. This is known as "reinforcing," which means increasing the likelihood of a behavior by responding to it in a manner pleasurable to the child. The child's behavior has also had an effect on the parent's behavior. The threatening behavior has made it less likely that the next time the parent will hold firm and not give in to the child. And when the child stops threatening after the parent acquiesces, it reinforces that behavior in the parent. As a result, these two systems are engaged in a predictable sequence: The parent initially tells the child no. The child predictably becomes aggressive, and the parent gives in to the child's demands, increasing the likelihood that the child will be aggressive next time. This is one example of how systems interact to maintain a child's behavior.

Let's say there are behavior problems at school. If the family is not aware of the behavior, the separate systems of the school and the family will not work together to change the behavior. Also, if the two systems, family and school, argue over who is to blame, interaction between the two sides may decrease, making it more likely that the child's behavior will continue while the two sides debate. However, if they are in frequent contact and work well together, they will be much more likely to be successful in altering the behavior. They may develop a strategy where school personnel report the child's behavior to the parents, who respond with praise or punishment based on the behavior. This coordinated effort is more effective than the two systems operating independently and without knowledge of each other's efforts.

## The Systems and Their Influence

There are many versions of the model shown in figure 1, which represents the major systems influencing your child's behavior. These systems are arranged in order of proximity, starting with those closest to your teen, which have the most direct influence. As the diagram shows, the family has the most influence. For this reason, it is most effective to begin with the family. Effective approaches use the family to create change in the other systems, such as school, peers, and neighborhood; remember, the various systems influence each other. By altering the systems and influences on your teen's behavior, you can effectively change his behavior, too.

# Changing Systems to Change Behavior

The concept of changing behavior by changing the environment around a youth is sometimes met with skepticism. However, your child's behavior already changes according to the environment. A child may be loud and aggressive with friends, but most kids do not behave that way at church, or with a grandmother, or around the police. Some environments support offensive behavior, while others do not. The goal is to change the environment around your child to one that no longer supports the behavior in question.

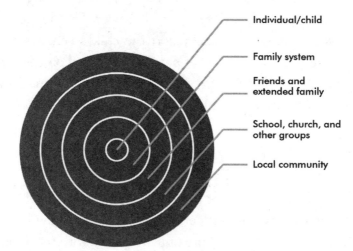

Figure 1 (Based on Bronfenbrenner 1979, 1988)

# Previous Delinquent Behavior

Though there are many ways of describing the predictors of delinquency over time, figure 2 provides perhaps the clearest and most concise synthesis of the data. It can also serve as a road map for your efforts to change your child's behavior. Note that previous delinquent behavior is a direct predictor of future offenses. If they did it before, they are likely to do it again. Unfortunately there is no way to "undo" a previous offense, so there is not much we can do about that one.

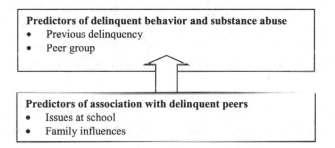

Figure 2 (Based on information in Elliott, Huizinga, and Ageton 1985 and Patterson, DeBaryshe, and Ramsey 1989)

# Peers

The other direct predictor of delinquent behavior, as shown in figure 2, is delinquent peers (Dishion et al. 1996; Prinstein and Dodge 2008), who encourage the behavior through their favorable attitudes toward and expressions of approval of it. Kids tend to operate in groups of friends and do things together. If your child is hanging around with kids who are committing offenses or using drugs, she's likely to do the same. If your child associates with kids who are playing sports or working on computers, she likely will not be stealing, getting high, or beating people up. If a group hangs out in front of a store, drinks, and harasses others, it makes sense that it would be more effective to remove your child from that situation rather than trying to explain that nice kids do not do such things.

The family is where this gets difficult, and it is crucial that you be honest with yourself. The research tells us that there are dynamics in families that predict the association with delinquent peers, which then predicts the behavior (see figure 2). There are many reasons for these dynamics, including the child's behavior. Let's first try to identify what patterns associated with delinquency exist in your family.

## Monitoring and Supervision

If you do not know where your child goes and with whom, it is much more likely that he can be found with delinquent kids. Lack of monitoring allows kids to have unsupervised time with other unsupervised kids, which provides opportunities for delinquent behavior.

In a similar way, it's unlikely that adult offenders will commit crimes under the watchful eye of a probation officer. However, when not in that person's presence, offenders are more likely to return to their previous behavior.

## Family Conflict

We also know that if things are not good at home, they are likely to be bad in other places. If your child has been raised with little warmth and a lot of conflict, he is likely to have learned behaviors like verbal and physical aggression that make him less likeable to other kids. Youths who are not easily accepted by others tend to hang around with kids in similar circumstances. This creates a group of aggressive teens who have all been rejected because of their aggression and lack of social skills (Miller-Johnson et al. 2002). This behavior is mutually reinforced through prompting behavior such as fighting or approval, and you now have a group of kids committing delinquent acts.

## School Behavior

Another factor that increases the likelihood of your child getting in trouble and associating with delinquent peers is difficulty in school. School activities allow youths to enhance social development; kids who are involved in school activities tend to be accepted by those who do not get into trouble. Those who are not active tend to socialize with others who are not active in school—yes, the delinquent group again. It usually is not leaders in student government who are arrested, although exceptions do occur. Those who look for opportunities to escape school by cutting class are much more likely to be involved in drugs and other delinquent activities (Vaughn et al. 2013).

## Poor Academics

It probably is not surprising that poor academic performance is linked to delinquent peer association. Those who do well academically tend to associate with others at the same level of performance, while those who shun academics also have a welcoming peer group—that's right, the club that frowns upon success and supports school failure and delinquency.

# Why Common Approaches Don't Work

You may now be puzzled about what all this means for you as a parent. Well, this tells us both what we should not do and what we should do. Let's start with what not to do, since you are undoubtedly considering all options. The research does not support working individually with your child. Though we can agree that your child's characteristics do have some influence, the research does not show that they are key factors in predicting delinquent behavior. Rather, the key factors are previous offenses and delinquent peers. Let's say that we chose to target the all-too-common attitude that acting out and breaking rules is cool, and were able to create some change in your child's perspective. But if your teen is surrounded by delinquent peers in an unsupervised situation, he is likely to drink and fight regardless of your efforts to change his attitude. I'm sure you can be persuasive, but I have a hard time picturing a child, in a situation where his friends are drinking, saying he no longer thinks it's a good idea. If on the other hand you take children, even those inclined toward offending, and place them in a situation where drinking and fighting are not acceptable to peers, you are less likely to see that behavior.

## Individual Therapy

This brings us to another difficulty in addressing you child as an individual: he is not motivated to change. He likes his attitude, and so do his friends—they all enjoy skipping school. I am not a gambler, but I would bet that as you read this, your child is not reading a book about how to stop drinking with friends and become a good student. A therapist meeting with him for one hour a week is not going to be able to talk him out of an attitude that he likes, one that his friends encourage for hours each day. He will learn what to say to impress you and school counselors and anyone else who attempts to change his behavior, leaving you with dashed hopes after the next call from the police. Though there are exceptions, individual therapy is not likely to generate lasting change in youths exhibiting delinquent behaviors. This frustrating ineffectiveness comes to you at a cost of anywhere from $100 to $150 per hour.

I will never forget an experience that illustrates my previous point about children learning what to say to counselors. I was working with a seventeen-year-old boy with an extensive history of drinking and drug use. I was energetic and hopeful during our sessions, and pleased when he told me he had learned his lesson. He clearly explained that he needed to make better choices and hang around with different people. Of course, I praised him for his wisdom, talked with him about his strategy for doing this, and discussed the circumstances that created his transformation. Not long after that, I witnessed this boy walking into a local bar with his friends. He knew what to tell me, but progress was minimal at best.

A 2013 study compared the outcomes for youths in New Jersey receiving functional family therapy with those receiving individual therapy or mentoring. The youths receiving functional family therapy showed significantly greater improvement across a wide variety of outcomes: "Specifically, only youth enrolled in FFT showed improved functioning in life domains, which include such areas as living situation, school behavior, achievement and attendance, and legal and vocational concerns" (Celinska, Ferrer, and Cheng 2013).

## Grouping Kids Together

The upcoming discussion will probably be upsetting to parents whose kids have been steered into programs that are currently popular. We know that the biggest predictor for delinquent behavior, other than prior delinquent behavior, is association with delinquent peers. In that case, what sense does it make to force delinquent kids to associate with each other? If you said none, you are correct. Nonetheless, we continually try intervention strategies that do just that. How often do you hear of kids being placed in group therapy, group homes, boot camp, and so on? These are very common treatment approaches in today's world. Whom do you think they are with in these programs? Group treatment centers and group homes are not filled with straight-A students and law-abiding kids who are there to meet young offenders and keep them straight. The kids who go into these programs are those committing offenses, and they are forced to meet and become friends with other young offenders—the very type of friendship that predicts delinquent behavior. Let me clarify that I am criticizing these approaches only for this specific group. Some of the treatment approaches being discussed are in fact helpful with other situations and challenges.

It satisfies our desire for justice (or vengeance) to see a drill sergeant yell at a thirteen-year-old on afternoon talk shows, but the truth is that there is no rigorous evidence to support these approaches. Before you defend these programs by citing the example of a cousin who has a friend whose nephew was helped by a boot camp program, I will concede that there are examples of each type being helpful to someone, but the research shows that this is not the case for most participants.

I will also concede that you can probably search the Internet and find articles that are apparently well researched promoting these programs. When seeking services, look for repeated clinical trials that show long-term outcomes, approaches that survive the scrutiny of peer review to be published in scholarly journals. The programs I consider effective have been recommended by the likes of the surgeon general (U.S. Department of Health & Human Services 1999; U.S. Public Health Service 2001), the National Institutes of Health (2006), the National Institute on Drug Abuse (2009), and the Office of Juvenile Justice and Delinquency Prevention (2007). When you are told that a program gets great results, ask yourself who published the results and where. Consider how they might measure results. The programs included in this discussion demonstrate significantly decreased rates of arrest for years following treatment.

# What About 12-Step Programs?

Since I am sure the question will be asked, let me say that the same reasoning outlined above also applies to programs such as Alcoholics Anonymous and Narcotics Anonymous. I am sure you know people who have been helped by these programs, and you yourself may even have been helped by these programs. However, research does not show them to be effective in treating substance abuse in juveniles (National Institute on Drug Abuse 2009).

Going back to the contributors to juvenile substance abuse, recall that the child's characteristics are not the biggest predictors of substance use. Therefore, targeting those is not likely to get the best result. We also know that grouping kids who are substance abusers is actually likely to promote substance use. Let's not forget that the kids who go into these programs typically do so to satisfy the court or their parents rather than out of a genuine desire to stop using. I worked with one mother who stopped her son from going to Narcotics Anonymous meetings because he was using on the premises while waiting for his ride home. As someone who has facilitated countless group therapy sessions with juveniles, I can tell you that they do learn the right things to say. I can also tell you that they whisper and hint to each other and giggle about the very behaviors they are denouncing.

# What You Can and Should Do

This brings us to what you can and should do. I cited some programs that have been shown to be effective by the Washington State Institute of Public Policy and Blueprints for Violence Prevention. Those programs are not yet available to all who need them, however. The purpose of this book is to tell you what strategies the research finds effective and how you as a parent can create change in your child's behavior.

To change delinquent behavior, it is essential to target the influences that contribute to or sustain the behavior. Specifically, you must examine and change contributors in the family, peer group, and school, possibly some elements in the neighborhood, and possibly your child. While I realize that this seems intimidating at first, I can tell you that these changes are attainable. I have worked on literally thousands of cases where parents have made these changes and been successful. You will be able to do it by utilizing skills and resources you have in these areas to create change, while I walk you through areas that may be new to you. The key is willingness. If you are sufficiently concerned, frustrated, angered, embarrassed, scared, disappointed, or hurt by the behavior of your child, the changes we discuss will seem trivial when compared to the thought of continuing along that path.

# PART 2

# What to Do

# Chapter 2

# Let's Talk About Parenting

I understand the depth of your frustration with your child's behavior and the fact that your efforts to date have not yielded the desired results. I have worked with thousands of families who had reached the limit and were ready to get rid of their children. I have seen all kinds of behavior in kids and can understand the anger, sadness, and embarrassment it brings to families. I know your situation is not easy; neither were those of any of the families I have encountered.

There is hope. I have seen families achieve remarkable changes in a child's behavior despite extremely bleak circumstances. I fondly remember a case where a boy was one step from going into a juvenile detention facility for a long time, and his family and friends were able to get the behavior under control enough for him to be accepted into a local college. Though you are frustrated, picking up this book and reading even to this point tells me that you and I share the same hope for you and your family. This chapter will address some common parenting challenges. It is my hope that it will leave you with some optimism and new ideas.

# Common Parental Concerns

**Do we really need to consider the whole family? It's my child who's the problem.**

While I agree that your child's behavior is the problem, parenting is one system that may contribute to a child's behavior. This does not mean you are guilty of bad parenting. It may be that your efforts are or would be successful with other kids, but they do not seem to be working with the child whose behavior led you to pick up this book.

In addition, parenting can be the most powerful influence in creating a change in behavior, and it is, luckily, the easiest one for you to change. Your efforts can then be directed to creating change in other areas of your child's life.

Your child's behavior may not seem to be a huge problem to her, but it is a big one for you and your family, and one you want to change. Together, you and others near your child can create a situation where your child will begin to see reasons to change her behavior.

**My child is old enough to know better.**

Depending on the age of your child, I most likely agree with you. However, your child is not making good decisions right now, and it is up to you to influence the decision-making process.

Remember when your child was an infant and you kept her away from electrical sockets, burners on the stove, or games in the street? During those times, your child was not making good decisions and needed your guidance to avoid serious consequences. Now you have taught your child those lessons, and playing in the street is no longer the relevant risk, but she is still making poor decisions, so it is still up to you to train her in the decision-making process. Before, a slap on the hand and a "no" were enough to teach the lesson. Now that she is older, the same principles still apply, but we need different methods of enforcement.

**My child should just behave. I should not have to do this!**

"Should" statements come in many forms and are applied to many topics. I have chosen to give them special attention because they create a lot of frustration when working with a child engaging in deliquent behavior, and can be a barrier to progress.

When you say, "My child should do this," you are essentially saying that your child should behave the way you think is best. However, your child does not see it the same way.

"Should" statements bump against the reality of the situation and stymie progress. The reality is that your child is not doing whatever it is that you think he should do, and being stuck on "should" keeps you from addressing the behavior because you have yet to acknowledge that (Persons 1989).

**Why is my child doing this to me?**

Your child is not "doing this to you" as a personal affront. Children behave the way they do because it is permitted and reinforced by a combination of elements in their surroundings. My guess is that your child either makes significant attempts to hide the behavior, or used to do so until he realized he could be more open. A person who intends to harm someone with a behavior typically does not attempt to have it go unnoticed.

# Parenting Styles

Psychologist Diana Baumrind (1966) has done extensive research on parenting. Through her research, she identified two basic domains of parenting: warmth and control. And she was able to identify four basic parenting styles based on the different levels of warmth and control. Let's start by making an honest assessment of your parenting style, as this will help you see the big picture of where you are and where you're headed.

# Authoritative Parenting

The children of authoritative parents perform well socially and have good relationships; they tend to be more self-reliant, are generally competent, and achieve academic success. What do these parents do? Authoritative parents positively reinforce appropriate behaviors in their children. While they set limits and offer punishments, they are not hostile or overly harsh in doing so, and they explain the rationale for the discipline. And while these parents are responsive to their children and attend to them, they do not give in to whining and nagging in order to pacify them. These parents may consider age-appropriate requests from their children, yet they also demand age-appropriate behaviors. Overall, these parents can be defined as having high warmth and high control.

# Permissive Parenting

Permissive parents show high warmth but little control. These are parents who express only acceptance of their children. They may attempt to reason with their children to get them to behave differently, but they are unlikely to wield parental power. They may allow the child to have more say in defining the norms or rules of the family rather than setting norms or rules in a top-down manner. Children of permissive parents may eventually display impulsive behavior and become difficult to control, especially in the face of disappointment. They may develop aggressive behavior and discover drugs and alcohol as they get older.

# Neglectful Parenting

Another group of parents that may display little control is neglectful or rejecting parents. While these parents are similar to permissive parents in that they have little control, they are different in that they do not share the same level of warmth and affection with their chilren. Neglectful parents remain predominantly uninvolved in parenting, putting little effort toward the emotional relationship with or discipline of their children. Children of neglectful parents often show emotional distress, which may manifest as delinquency and drug use.

## Authoritarian Parenting

Authoritarian parents maintain high levels of behavioral control over their children yet have low levels of warmth. They stress absolute obedience and use harsh discipline to achieve that obedience. Authoritarian parents tend to disregard a child's input in decisions and insist on unquestioning obedience. Children of these parents are frequently stressed, irritable, and hostile, and they may have low self-confidence. This may result in aggression, social withdrawal, and other delinquent behaviors as children grow older.

## Your Style

If you are able to identify where you fall in these categories, it may suggest which direction you need to head in your parenting strategy. The ideal would be to move toward an authoritative parenting style. You may need to add some rules and discipline, or remove some; you may need to attend to your relationship with your child, or allow your child to experience some hardship through consequences or not getting her way. Please remember that these categories are broad generalizations. They are not intended to be absolute truths or laws when determining the behavior and social adjustment of children. However, they can be helpful in identifying the road ahead as you attempt to gain control your child's behavior.

It is also important to combat a common misperception. People often think automatically that the way to change a child's behavior is to be tougher and make the child suffer consequences. While appropriate consequences are important, that is not the correct answer in every case. If the child has already lost everything and has nothing to gain by behaving appropriately, further consequences are not likely to work. Note that authoritative parents provide consequences and expect their children to follow rules, but they also provide praise and reinforcement, which are very powerful in teaching your child to behave. Authoritarian parents offer little in the way of reinforcement and praise, and their children frequently find themselves in trouble.

## Steven

I worked with the family of a boy we will call Steven. The family was so frustrated by his behavior that they were ready to have him removed from the home, which was the next step legally. To deal with his truancy, we tried to find a punishment for Steven that would be meaningful enough to get him to go to school. After several unsuccessful attempts, the family was asked if they could think of anything else they could remove. The family responded that they had tried everything and removed everything they could imagine. Upon closer inspection, the family had indeed taken away everything that brought enjoyment to Steven's life. Steven had been punished repeatedly and seemingly randomly; his home lacked warmth and support. His room was bare, with only a mattress on the floor. They could take nothing else, and there was little they could do to influence his behavior, or so they thought. We then initiated a plan to help the family move to a more authoritative style. We developed a system that would allow him to earn privileges or the return of belongings for specific behavior. We brought Steven into the conversation regarding things he wanted to earn.

Surprisingly, what Steven most wanted was an outing with an older brother who no longer lived in the house. The older brother agreed, and a system was created whereby Steven could earn the outing based on school attendance and behavior. As Steven began to work toward this privilege, we allowed him to earn back privileges and items he had previously lost. The family began to recognize the progress and show more warmth while having appropriate expectations. Within weeks, Steven's school attendance increased to where he was meeting expectations and was no longer considered truant.

Parents are only one of many influences on a child's behavior, but they happen to be the one with the most power. Parents differ in many ways—from their style of relationship with their kids to their method of discipline. Though different approaches can be effective, and what works with one child may not work with the next, the research tells us that an authoritative parenting style, exhibiting high warmth and high control, is the most likely to lead to the desired behaviors. An examination of your style can be instructive in developing your strategy, whether that includes increasing efforts at discipline or increasing the warmth in the home.

# Chapter 3

# The Rules of the House

Setting the rules for your house is essential. If you have expectations for your child's behavior, she needs to know what they are. If the rules are not clear or not consistent, she will not know the standards and will experience your response to her behavior as arbitrary. Establishing and enforcing clear rules teaches children about limits and acceptable behavior. It also provides the framework in which they learn to manage their emotions in response to life's disappointments. The boundaries and expectations instill the discipline children will need to be successful later in life. For many teens, enforcement of rules is crucial, as it sets boundaries to keep them safe when they aren't making good choices for themselves.

Because parenting is one of many influences on your child's behavior, it is clear that effective rules will be essential to your effort to change your child's behavior, whether that involves school attendance or where your child goes on Friday night. Effective rules will also help you address behavior that may endanger your child or put her at risk for arrest.

# Creating the Rules

According to Richard Munger's *Rules for Unruly Children* (1999), the first step in creating rules is to list your child's problem behaviors. Though the list may be long, choose three or four behaviors that are the most important to target. I recommend prioritizing behaviors that pose a safety risk as well as those that may lead to legal trouble. The reason for limiting the number is that for a rule to be effective, it must be enforced consistently, and it will be very difficult for you to enforce ten rules.

After you have your list, you are ready to create the rules. It is important that the rules be very specific and the expected behaviors clearly defined. Our young delinquents are very good lawyers, so there can be no room for discussion as to whether a rule has been broken. For example, you may have a rule that your child must clean his room. In many cases, a child's definition of a clean room is different from your definition, which creates room for discussion about whether the expectation has been met. In this rule, it would be more helpful to specify that your child must clean his room each day by a given time, and cleaning the room means that the bed is made, sporting equipment is in the closet, dirty clothes are in the hamper, and so on.

# Consistent Enforcement

To be effective, rules must be enforced each time they are violated. A good example is speed limits. I'm sure some of you occasionally drive faster than the speed limit, and some of you may do so frequently. You know the speed limit is a rule, and you know police officers will enforce it if they see you speeding. However, it is impossible for them to watch you at all times, so you often break the law without receiving a ticket. For this reason, you do not receive tickets often enough to change your driving habits. If, however, your car signaled highway patrol each time you crossed the speed limit, the result being a $200 ticket, you would be more likely to observe speed limits. The same is true for rules of the house. If you do not enforce the rule consistently, it will not change your child's behavior.

# Find the Loopholes

Take into consideration any possible loopholes and make adjustments to fill those loopholes (Munger 1999). For example, if you have a rule stating that your child must be home by 10 p.m., you may need to specify that you mean 10 p.m. by the clock on the wall in the kitchen. If not, you may find yourself in a debate when your child realizes that two clocks are fifteen minutes apart, possibly on purpose. To eliminate loopholes, take some time to consider how your child might attempt to manipulate the rule.

# Establish Consequences

Once you have established rules, it is time to establish the consequences (punishment) that you will link to each rule as well as reinforcements (rewards) that may be earned for compliance. We'll start with the consequences. (Throughout this book, there will be occasions where I use the word "consequence" as a substitute for "punishment." Though the terms are not necessarily equivalent, I do so to remind parents who may be uncomfortable implementing punishment that the child is facing the punishment as a result of rule violations.) Many parents say they cannot think of any consequence for an inappropriate behavior. Take a look around your house and consider the things that bring pleasure to your child's life, as well as any privileges he has—the majority of what you see is fair game. But there are a few limits. I do not advocate removing the basic needs of life. You should not consider taking away food, shelter, or necessary clothing, and you should never take away the love of a parent.

## Basic Needs

Let's talk about what I mean when I say that basic needs like food, shelter, and clothing are not to be removed as a punishment. When I refer to basic needs, I mean that once these needs are adequately met, anything else is a luxury. Your child needs nutritious food, but he does not need snacks, fast food, pizza, or other favorites. Your child needs shoes, but he does not need trendy shoes with a triple-digit price tag. Your child needs a warm coat, but fashion is not a basic need. I'm sure you're starting to get the picture. Trendy clothes and image can be very important for teens, but the things that go into a fashionable image are not basic needs. Accordingly, they make an excellent consequence for inappropriate behavior. Removing them from a child's closet is frequently a powerful way to gain his attention, and children are frequently willing to comply in exchange for the return of some clothes.

## Positive Activities

I do not advocate taking away positive activities like sports, school clubs, or music (unless it's a drug-abusing garage band). You may question why I resist taking away a child's privilege of playing sports. Remember how important a child's peers are in delinquency. Prosocial activities like sports and clubs provide your child with an opportunity to grow and develop socially and to form friendships with kids who are not getting into trouble. If you remove these activities, your child may begin to turn toward peer groups that are not involved in prosocial activities—that's right, the delinquents.

Outside these limitations, anything else your child enjoys may be used as either a consequence or a reward. Consider favorite electronics, freedoms, clothing, foods, or any other item or privilege that would be meaningful to your child.

# Amy

I worked with the family of a girl we will call Amy. Amy was aggressive and refused to follow the rules of the house. When her mother confronted her with rule violations, Amy became loud and threatening, thus aborting her mother's attempt to gain control of the behavior. We worked with her mother to identify a consequence that would be meaningful enough to influence Amy's behavior, but either the items or privileges we tried were not meaningful enough or her mother was not able to enforce them. After careful consideration, we concluded that Amy's looks and image were dear to her and developed a consequence targeting her desire to always look her best. Amy's mother explained that Amy's behavior was not going to be tolerated and if she were to violate the rules again, she could be sure of receiving a consequence. As expected, Amy violated the rules that very evening. While she was out, Amy's mother confiscated her makeup, lotions, hair products, and perfume. When Amy arrived home, she found an empty bathroom. Needless to say, this was very upsetting to her and proved an effective method of changing her behavior.

You may have guessed that Amy was not warned of the specific consequence that her mother was going to use. In most cases, parents inform the child of the consequence for noncompliance, but this strategy may be altered if necessary. In this case, we knew that if Amy was warned ahead of time, she would hide her makeup, defeating our strategy.

# More Significant Consequences

Some behavior may require more severe consequences, particularly when the behavior presents a significant safety risk, such as assaulting people or roaming the streets for days at a time. For example, I have had parents file police reports, press charges, have their child spend the night in jail, and worse. Such consequences should be carefully planned and should not include any safety risk. There are also many cases in which these strategies would not be advisable. Consider that your child may enter the juvenile justice system, and you may lose control. In addition, arrest may place the child in the company of delinquent peers. Another concern is that the police may be seen as the ones in control, rather than you. If your child needs to be taken off the street for safety reasons, you could alleviate some of these concerns by speaking with the police in advance to see if they would support your child only spending a night or a few days in confinement. You should also be very clear, and have the arresting officer be very clear, that the arrest resulted from your decision to no longer tolerate the behavior.

## James

James was continually late for school, when he attended, and was at risk of being expelled. Like many teenagers, James put on a tough image and was embarrassed by the mere existence of his parents. One day his mother informed him that the next time the school told her he had failed to arrive on time, she would take him to school herself to make sure he got there when he was supposed to. As usual, James was late that very day. The next morning, his mother drove him to school and walked him into the building wearing her robe, slippers, and curlers in her hair. For

James, it was significant enough to make him not want to risk such an entrance the following day.

This example makes clear that the parental response needs to be tailored to the specific child. Many children would not be fazed by such an escort and might find it humorous.

## Chores as a Consequence

Some parents find that assigning additional household chores makes an effective consequence. Your child can wash dishes, clean toilets, mow the lawn, or do any chores you desire. If he washed the dishes by hand yesterday and got into another argument with the teacher today, you are free to have him wash the dishes again today or complete another chore from your to-do list. This approach has the added benefit of being helpful to the parents. However, there are some drawbacks. First, you must have a plan in place in case your child decides not to do the chores. Be prepared with an additional consequence that you can enforce until he complies. You must also consider how the chores compare with the offense. For example, a teenager might gladly exchange an hour of mowing the lawn for a chance to skip school for a day. For this strategy to work, the chores must be significant enough to match the severity and perceived benefit of the behavior.

## Useful Consequences for Working Parents

For parents who are not able to be home at all times or have difficulty supervising a child's coming and goings, consequences like grounding or an earlier curfew may not be enforceable. In these situations, parents are frequently more successful in denying access to an item that can be removed. For example, many parents tell a child they are not allowed to use computer games or computers and enforce this by taking the machine or power cords with them. Bicycles can be locked or tires removed. Stereos and other devices allow for simple removal of the item or key parts. Parents can also remove phones, or stop payment on a contract, if a child refuses to hand over the phone. A weekly allowance can be denied by not giving it to the child. There are endless possibilities, but the key is to find something that your child values and that you are able to enforce restricted access to.

# Link Consequences to Behavior

Once you have established the possible consequences and rewards, attach a consequence to each target behavior, and present it to your child so the expectations are clear. It is important to avoid overlapping consequences and rewards. For example, you may decide that your child is not to go out on the weekend if she skips school. Another rule may state that if she cleans the house, she can stay out thirty minutes later than usual. Under this system, your child could skip school, clean the house, and then argue that not only should she be allowed to go out but she should be allowed to stay out thirty minutes later than usual. This example highlights a common mistake and shows the importance of attaching distinct contingencies to each rule.

## Common Parental Concerns

### I feel guilty taking away my child's belongings.

Most parents do not like to punish their children because they love them and do not want to see them unhappy. Reluctance is normal, but it should not stop you from enforcing rules. Would you rather your child suffer these consequences or have him face those imposed by society? There will be consequences either way. And your child will certainly not be happy if he is hurt or incarcerated.

Consider it this way: All these rewards are available to your child. She will decide to do what's necessary to earn any rewards that are important to her. You have explained the expectations; she must decide whether to follow them.

Another way of looking at it is that your child begins each day with a blank slate. She can either earn these items or privileges or she can choose not to earn them. That's the way most people's jobs work, after all. You begin the day having not made any money; you can choose to go to work, meet the expectations, and earn money as a result, or you can miss work and not earn anything.

### I don't want my child to be mad at me.

Your child has been mad at you before and will be mad at you again. It is not fun, but it is not the end of the world either. What are the results of your efforts not to anger your child? Your child still gets angry and still gets over it like everyone else. If you were following a behavior plan, you might also change your child's behavior.

### I want to have a good relationship with my child.

Your relationship with your child is already strained if you're reading this book. Wouldn't you have a better relationship with your child if she was behaving according to your expectations—attending school, not using drugs, and not being aggressive? What is the future of your relationship if your child ends up behind bars, hospitalized, on drugs, or worse? How will she feel when she realizes that you did not provide her with guidance when she really needed it?

### My child knows the rules and should just follow them.

A rule without enforcement is not a rule; it is merely a suggestion. If your child does not like the suggestion, she will do as she pleases, having no reason to behave differently. In addition, this thought pattern keeps you from moving forward and addressing the reality that she is not following the rules.

# Reinforcing Desired Behavior

Consequences are made even more powerful when combined with reinforcement. Some parents impose consequences as well as allowing their children to earn additional privileges or rewards. Parents who are reluctant to remove a privilege sometimes find it easier to have a child start with nothing at the beginning of each day and earn privileges by complying with the rules.

## Your Child's Interests

To begin identifying rewards, it is helpful to identify activities or objects your child enjoys. You may also want to consider things your child used to enjoy prior to the start of the problematic behavior. In addition, listen for any interests your child might have recently developed. The most obvious way to gather ideas, though, is to ask your child. The reward is more likely to work if you give her the opportunity to choose it. However, parents have the final say. The item or privilege must be something you are comfortable with and willing and able to provide.

## Special Time

You may also want to consider whether your child might like to spend additional time with someone. Is there an extended family member, an older sibling, or a neighbor who would be willing to spend some special time with your child as a reward for good behavior? In two cases that come immediately to my mind, this was a powerful reinforcement. In one case, a child was allowed to ride go-carts with an uncle on the weekend if he attended school all week. In another case—Steven's, mentioned in the previous chapter—a child spent time with an older sibling in exchange for completing homework and remaining at school all day.

## Places and Activities

Children often have places they want to go or activities they enjoy. Access or transportation to those places can be important rewards. As a word of caution, it is important to do due diligence on the places or activities your child enjoys; otherwise, you may be providing transportation to meet drug-abusing peers.

## Money

Avoid giving money to a child who may be using alcohol or drugs. If your child wants to buy something, you can use a system of tokens with a given value to track earnings, and then purchase the approved item for her when enough has been accrued. Alternatively, create a daily checklist and check items off as she earns points toward the desired item. This type of system is beneficial when your child wishes to earn a larger item or privilege. It is also an effective method in situations where inappropriate behavior occurs frequently because tokens or points can easily be applied to small increments of time, as will be described in the next section.

## Token Economy

To use these systems effectively, make each behavior worth a specified number of points. For example, if verbal aggression is one of the targeted behaviors, the child might earn twenty-five points for making it through the day without verbal aggression. If the behavior normally occurs more frequently, you may give points based on a set number of hours. The time frame for earning points depends on the frequency of the behavior. You want him to have to go longer than usual but not so long as to be unrealistic. As the behavior begins to be more controlled, you can lengthen the time period of compliance needed to get the points.

For example, say you give a favorite game a value of 250 points. You then break your child's day into five time periods, each worth five points. If he goes for the designated time period without being verbally aggressive, he earns the five points. If he avoids the behavior for the entire day, he earns twenty-five points; after ten days, he earns the game. After that, you might increase the time period by an hour. In the case of truancy, if your child has not been to school in two weeks, you might let him win points for each day of attendance; if he typically misses only one day a week, you might let him earn points for attending every day for a week.

## Common Parental Concerns

### My child has not done anything special to deserve a reward.

The goal is not for your child to accomplish extraordinary acts of kindness that improve the plight of humanity. The goal is for him to simply not do whatever problematic behavior is being targeted. Of course, we also want your child to begin doing whatever new behaviors are identified. He may still look angry and not want to talk to you, but if he accomplishes the goal you set—say, making curfew—he should get the reward. Even if you are upset with him for some other reason, you must make good on the reward, or you cannot expect him to follow the rules you have established.

**I should not have to bribe my child.**

We humans naturally repeat things that get a pleasant response, whether it's praise at work or laughter in social settings. It is quite likely that your child's less desirable behaviors are getting her some response that she likes. It is important to ensure that the responses to appropriate behavior be more pleasurable to her than the response to her current behavior. If the delinquent behavior brings punishment and the desired behavior brings a reward, we can expect behavior to change. Note that these rewards aren't bribes. What you are doing is training your child to behave in ways that are more socially acceptable. A bribe typically involves payment for a less acceptable behavior.

**My child says she does not care about any of the rewards and consequences and will not participate.**

Many parents give up when the child refuses to comply. If you give up, your child learns that she can undermine your attempts simply by expressing disapproval. Your child does care. Pretending not to care is a common method children use, and it almost worked on you. Your child may say she is not interested or does not care. If she does, great—then you should have no problems enforcing the rules. Enforce them well, with meaningful consequences and rewards, and you'll find your child does care.

# **Exercise:** Develop the Rules

1. *Develop a list of behaviors that you find problematic, and narrow the list to the top three or four.*

2. *Write a rule for each behavior, being careful to define subjective terms and to close any loopholes.*

3.  Determine how you will monitor your child's behavior.

4.  Take an inventory of items or privileges that may be used as a reward or punishment for each identified behavior. Make sure you will be able to effectively control the item or privilege.

5.  Create a table or chart linking a privilege to each behavior, then rate them according to perceived value and significance of the behavior.

# Presenting the Rules

Once you have established the rules and linked a consequence to each, present them to your child. You may present them with rewards you yourself have established or seek your child's input. This will be a significant change in the house, and it's only fair to tell your child that changes are being made. For the conversation to go well, ask to speak with your child at a time when there is no open conflict. Consider the words you plan to use. For example, you might say, "We love you and are concerned that some of your behavior is beginning to get you into significant trouble and danger. Because we do not want to see that happen, we are going to begin enforcing some rules around the house. Those rules will be _____. If you follow the rules, you can earn _____ , and if you choose not to follow them, _____ will be the consequence. We really hope you choose to earn the privileges and that you will ask for help if you need it."

It's highly unlikely that your child is going to thank you at the end of this conversation. There is a strong possibility that he will become angry or show little reaction. Regardless of the response, do not be swayed. This approach does not require your child's consent. You are trying to move  away from letting your child have so much power in the home. This program simply requires you to proceed consistently. If your child responds angrily or does not respond, simply say, "It's your choice," and leave the room.

# Enforcement

There are several key elements to effective implementation of rules. In an earlier discussion, we mentioned the importance of consistency. Each rule must be enforced consistently. I have had parents say that the child "knows the rules," or "I told him what to do." I will give you the same response I gave them: "Without enforcement, a rule is only a suggestion." You should not expect your child to follow the rules just because you stated them; otherwise, you would not be in the present situation. If there has been no consistent enforcement, your child has no reason to follow rules. And for your rules to be meaningful, your child must experience consequences.

This next point may come as a welcome concept but it can be difficult to implement: I do not want you to argue with your child. This bit of advice falls into the category of working smarter, not harder. When you present a consequence to your child, becoming emotional or arguing works against you. Deliver the news in an even, matter-of-fact, businesslike tone of voice. There is no reason to argue. You have presented the rules and consequences, and your child has made a choice. Simply state that he has violated the rule and thus the consequence will be given. You may be angry and want to react, perhaps by yelling. Most likely, you have yelled before, and your yelling has not resulted in lasting behavior change. Only enforcement of the rules will lead to change. In addition, the more yelling and arguing you do, the more opportunity you give your little lawyer to engage you in debate. In addition, yelling makes it more likely that conflict will erupt, which also lowers your chances of success. There is no reason to be pulled into a debate with your child. Commit this to memory:

> *Child:*    Mom, that's not fair.
>
> *Mom:*    You broke the rule and this is the consequence.
>
> *Child:*    You're a #*@#! All my friends are going.
>
> *Mom:*    I understand that you want to go, but you broke the rule and this is the consequence. (*Leaves the room.*)

When giving a reward, however, it is entirely acceptable to speak more and engage in more discussion. You may offer as much praise as your child will tolerate.

# Troubleshooting

Before starting your program, it is important to understand that behaviors frequently escalate for a short time before they improve. Frequently, parents enforce a rule and the child has a strong reaction, leading the surprised parents to conclude that the rule did not work. They return to their previous approach feeling more defeated and powerless than ever. If this happens, you have increased the likelihood of the child exhibiting that behavior in the future. It is crucial to remain consistent with your enforcement even when the behavior continues or escalates. Let's examine the reason for this.

## Enforcing Limits Despite the Reaction

When a child's reaction to a limit makes the parent give up, the child's reaction is reinforced. When the parent later tries to enforce the rule, the child will react in the way that has been successful in the past: an outburst. This outburst will likely be even greater because the parent has raised the stakes. However, if the parent responds to the outburst with an additional consequence, the original limit stands and the outburst is also punished, making future occurrences less likely.

For example, a child comes home forty-five minutes after curfew. His mother responds by telling him that he is not allowed to watch television for the evening. The child immediately has a loud and emotional outburst of the type that used to get him his way. His mother now explains that if the outburst continues, he will also lose access to the telephone. In many cases, the child will test this with an additional outburst; the parent must then remove the telephone. Initially, this may yield quite a series of outbursts, but if the parents meet each of the child's escalations by escalating their response, the behavior will change over time.

## Are the Consequences Meaningful?

If, over time, you do not see a change in behavior, you may want to consider the strength of your consequences and reinforcements. For a consequence or reinforcement to be successful, it must be meaningful to the child. In addition, the desire for that object or privilege must not be easily replaced. For example, if you restrict your child's access to computer games but he is allowed to go to a friend's house where they play computer games for hours, your denying him the games is meaningless. In this situation, you have several options. You could find another consequence. You might also contact the friend's parents and ask that your child not be allowed to play the games at his house. The most severe possibility is to tell your child, when he misbehaves, that he must not need his games so you will start to get rid of them one by one after a certain period of noncompliance. The available options are limited only by your imagination, and the guidelines for consequences given earlier in this chapter. To this end, you may want to add a clause at the end of your rules stating that you have the right to alter consequences as you deem necessary. This will avoid allowing your young lawyer to argue that you are violating the agreement.

## Preparing for the Predictable Response

Another difficulty parents often face is a result of not being prepared for the child's response. It is your job to be prepared to meet your child's response with one of your own. Do you remember Amy? We suspected that when her mother confiscated her makeup, Amy would delve into her mother's stock, so we advised her mother to lock up her own makeup. Amy was then faced with the reality of life without makeup. It is a good idea to assume that your child will try to work around the consequence or to escalate the situation.

### Mandy

Mandy's mother was preparing to present her with the final rules for good behavior after seeking her input. Mandy had not welcomed the ideas, so we knew her response to the rules was not going to be favorable. Her mother thought Mandy would probably rip up the list of rules once it was presented to her. When Mandy tried to do as predicted, she found that her mother had laminated it.

### Linda

Linda was a fourteen-year-old with a fondness for nightlife. Her parents began to apply a curfew with significant consequences and reinforcements. They suspected that

Linda would comply with the curfew only to sneak out once they had gone to bed. For a few nights, her father rigged Linda's window with an alarm and then slept in a sleeping bag outside her room. After tripping over her father and receiving a more significant consequence for her attempt to sneak out, she began to see the value of complying with the curfew.

There are times when a consequence fails because the child walks out of the house. If this occurs, several options are available to you. You may enlist someone else's help in bringing the child home. This might be a family member with a good relationship with the child, a neighbor, a friend's parents, or the police. We will discuss this approach later.

A second option would be to tell your child that leaving home to avoid a consequence will result in a more significant consequence upon her return. This would be appropriate if she leaves and returns home in a reasonable amount of time. If you choose this option, your next consequence needs to be one that can effectively be enforced.

A third option is available for more extreme cases. Remember, it is essential to have your child available to face the consequences you provide, or your effort and planning will be for naught. If your child does not spend much time at home or leaves for extended periods, one solution is to remove his clothes from his room and confiscate the clothes he has on when he returns home to shower. I do not mean that you should force your child to walk around the house in the nude; rather, you should leave him with just enough to reasonably cover himself. This way, at the very least, your child will be easy to identify if he decides to leave again. In most cases he will simply stay home. Once he has completed the punishment, he may earn the return of his garments. Again, this is certainly a more extreme approach and should only be used in cases where it's warranted by the severity of the behavior. The safety risk of a child being on the streets late at night in places where illegal activity occurs is significant enough to resort to this more extreme approach if others have not worked.

## Common Parental Concerns

**I am afraid that my child will attack me physically if I try to impose these consequences.**

Unfortunately, this can be a real threat for some people. Let me clearly state that your safety should always come first. If you think an assault is imminent, call the police immediately. There will be further discussion of safety in chapter 6.

**This is too much for me (us) to manage.**

Many parents find it difficult to make these changes, particularly if there are other children, jobs, or similar factors. These changes are not easy, and you will need support. This is why it is important to assemble a team of supportive friends, family members, and coworkers early in the process. There will be further discussion of your team in chapter 7.

# **Exercise:** Plan to Present the Rules

1. *Plan the time, place, and attendees for a conversation in which you will present the new rules to your child.*

2. *Identify who will be the best person to state the rules, and plan exactly how the rules will be presented.*

3. *You may seek your child's input on possible rewards and rules where there is some flexibility, such as curfew, but you have the final say.*

4.  *Predict how your child will respond, and plan your response (leave the room, have someone intervene, offer encouragement).*

5.  *Practice.*

# How Long Do I Have to Do This?

Parents often gain some success by consistently enforcing limits only to have the troublesome behavior return when they relax their effort. This leaves them wondering if they will have to follow such a plan forever. It is not necessary to punish each occurrence of the inappropriate behavior or reward each occurrence of the appropriate behavior for all eternity. However, if you stop rewarding or punishing as appropriate very suddenly, it is likely that the old behavior patterns will return. It is also true that if you repeat the same reward on a daily basis, it will lose its power.

It is best to decrease the frequency of rewarding a behavior using a process called "thinning." Thinning gradually reduces the frequency of the reward so that the behavior is rewarded on an intermittent basis, making it more likely to continue. The best example of this is in the popularity of slot machines. People know they will not win with each pull of the arm, but they do not know when the next jackpot will happen. They continue to play for hours at a time though they are only reinforced by occasional small winnings. The same principle applies when teaching your child new behaviors. Once he has begun to exhibit the behavior consistently, you may begin to alter the reward schedule and "thin" the reinforcement over time. Explain to your child that he is doing so well that he no longer needs a reward each time. The praise and success experienced will begin to fill in as a reward, just as it does for other successful people, but you can continue to spontaneously provide deliberate reinforcement for good behavior. If the behavior begins to escalate, do not see this as failure. Go back to what you were doing to regain success, moderating as necessary. One instance of being tardy to school requires a consequence but not one of the same intensity as the one you gave when your child skipped school for four days at a time. If you do see your child reverting to old behaviors full force, feel free to increase the frequency of rewards and punishment as necessary.

As you can see, there are many components to the essential process of enforcing household rules. This can be much more difficult than it sounds, particularly with a child who's already getting into trouble, but you can do it. Carefully walk through each step to be absolutely clear on what you plan to do, then practice before moving forward. There can be an element of trial and error in becoming effective, but each attempt will provide you with new information. Dissect all your attempts, both successful and unsuccessful, to identify what made the strategy work or what got in the way. If you have not been as successful as hoped, look through the chapter and see if you are able to identify or develop a strategy to address the problem. If you have been successful, plan to incorporate the crucial elements into future attempts.

# Chapter 4

# "Where Are You Going?"

To have any chance of enforcing rules and changing their children's behavior, parents must know where their children go, who their friends are, and what they do together. This is absolutely essential to success. You cannot enforce rules if you do not know whether or when they are being broken. In addition, most truly delinquent behaviors are committed in places that lack adequate supervision and with a group of people who accept or applaud that behavior. If you hope to change it, your child needs to be in places where he is monitored and with people who do not condone criminal behavior.

When your child exhibits such behavior as drug or alcohol use, property destruction, or fighting, this should immediately tell you that your child was not being supervised appropriately; that he was out of sight of people in authority who would not tolerate that behavior. Similarly, considering the influence of peers, if your child has a peer group who engages in problem behavior, their activities should be supervised accordingly. I can already hear you saying that you will not be able to follow your child twenty-four hours a day. No problem—I do not expect that. However, you or someone who is willing to help needs to know where your child is and what he is doing. This chapter will help you establish a strategy.

# Providing the Right Level of Monitoring

The amount of supervision needed to change your child's behavior is not dictated by your work schedule or your play schedule. The extent of detail required and the intensity of your monitoring efforts are solely dependent upon the intensity of your child's behaviors and what it will take for you to be successful. Having said that, it is possible that your child needs almost constant supervision. As I said previously, I do not expect you to have your child in sight at all times, but if observation is required for a period of time, it is important to make sure that either you or a surrogate is able to monitor.

## Adam

Adam was sneaky and would leave in the morning but not arrive at school. On days when he did arrive, he would cut out early, going various places where he was able to use drugs and engage in other problematic behavior. Adam's parents initially tried to establish a routine where they could check on him at key times of the day. However, since both parents worked, loopholes were readily available. Adam's father then called another family meeting, but this one was not the same as the others. This time, he invited the extended family, including his siblings and their spouses. During the meeting, he explained that he and his wife were working to keep Adam in school and to supervise him after school. The family created a document that listed each hour of the day for each day of the week. The family members pooled their efforts to make sure someone was responsible for knowing where Adam was at each hour of the day. One person drove him to school, where Adam was delivered to a member of the school staff. The school staff agreed that if Adam left school during the day, they would contact the identified family member. After school, Adam was handed off to the family member assigned to pick him up that afternoon. Adam spent some days working with his uncle at a garage; other days were spent with other relatives. But there was no time when Adam did not have supervision. Family members knew when they were responsible and who was responsible at other times, which allowed for effective communication. If Adam met the family requirements for the week, he was allowed to spend the weekend riding four-wheelers with his cousins. If not, he would spend his weekend doing chores. In this way, Adam's parents were able to closely monitor Adam's behavior even though they were too busy to do so on their own.

# Regina

Regina's family created a monitoring plan much like Adam's. Her behavior included not only skipping school but drug use and dealing. By process of elimination, we figured out that Regina was acquiring drugs at school. To combat this problem, her family created an extensive monitoring plan that included the school staff. The school staff watched where she sat to keep her away from problematic peers and followed her as she moved between classes. In addition, Regina's mother searched her pockets before dropping her off at school and when she returned. Her mother also made random visits to school to search her and make sure she had not acquired drugs. With such close supervision, Regina and her friends seem to have agreed that the level of risk was not worth continuing her behavior.

# Strategies for Monitoring

Having seen a couple of the more extreme examples, let's look at some of the more common strategies.

## Collaborate with Other Parents

Perhaps the most obvious strategy is to develop a collaborative relationship with the parents of your child's friends. This will allow you to verify much of the information provided by your teen. In addition, it will allow you to ensure that his activities are monitored when he says he is going to someone's house by making a simple phone call to see that a parent is home. You should make use of this resource frequently. If your child says he is going to Bill's house, call Bill's parents to verify this and to make sure it is a supervised situation. I would also suggest getting to know Bill's parents or driving by their house to make sure that there is proper supervision and that they are not allowing children to have parties.

## Collaborate with the Staff at Recreation Centers

The same due diligence should be exercised if your child begins to get involved in activities at a local recreation center. We certainly hope such activities, whether sports, art classes, or any other activity, are well supervised. If so, this supervised activity can be a great method of monitoring while engaging your child in a positive activity. However, far too many community centers serve as prime locations for drug activity. If your child spends time at such a center, it is to your benefit to enlist a person there to serve as an additional set of eyes.

# Identify Approved Places

Another common strategy for busy parents is to identify a few locales that meet your approval. This may include friends' homes where you know the friends and trust the supervision, community centers where the premises and activities are well monitored, or any other setting where you know the people, have spoken with them about the plan, and are certain that there will be effective supervision. Tell your child that she needs to be at such an approved location, and that any violation will be taken to mean that she was not in an approved place. This allows you to monitor from work by making a few phone calls to predetermined places.

# Reach Out to the Local Police

If your child is really getting into trouble, it is quite possible that the local police know where she spends her free time. Police have a difficult job and are on the lookout for allies, so they may welcome your effort to rid their area of one more youthful offender. I have had several cases where busy parents have reached out to police officers who patrol their area. These parents provided the officers with their children's names and pictures and asked the officers to notify them if the child was seen in a less than desirable location. Police may also be helpful in evaluating places that your child can spend their time. I suggest asking them about the activities that go on at any location you may be considering, as well as where youths who are not getting into trouble tend to spend their time.

# Work with the School Staff

The school staff may also be a good source of information. An abundance of information flows through the faculty and staff; they frequently overhear conversations among youths walking the halls or sitting in the classrooms or cafeteria. If you ask, you may be able to find out about your child's whereabouts over the weekend or what he did at a big party. You may also find out information about upcoming events that would be helpful in assessing whether to allow your child to attend. School staff may know where your teen might be in the afternoon or be able to tell you where youths without problem behaviors are spending their time.

## Watch Where Teens Go

A sure way to monitor the whereabouts of your teen is to go places with him or, if necessary, follow him when he leaves the house. Obviously this requires time that some parents do not have, but it does have several benefits. The first is that you see where he goes. In addition, you may gain information about his peer group and the activities of its members. Following your child can also serve as a punishing consequence for a child who does not tell you where he plans to go. Remember the discussion about image being important to teens? Not many want to arrive at the local hangout accompanied by parents with the express purpose of checking to see where they go and meeting their friends.

## Get Help from Local Businesses and the Community

Teens frequently congregate around such businesses as pool halls or convenience stores. Through some simple investigation, you can probably locate the most popular locales. If a group of troublesome youths associates around a business, it is likely that they are not the desired clientele of the business. Business owners and employees may appreciate your effort to reduce by one the number of teens loitering on the premises. Introduce yourself to people at the business; ask if they know your child, and be prepared to provide a picture. If the activities and the group of kids are not to your liking, encourage the employees and the manager to call you if they see your teen. Upon receiving the call, you can either retrieve your child or provide a consequence upon his return home. That decision should be based upon the severity of the behavior and your level of concern about his peers.

The same type of outreach you use with business owners can be used with other members of the community. Neighbors and others in the community frequently have a great deal of information about what goes on in the area and where teens hang out. Many would gladly share information, but they will not get involved until asked. If you really want to know where your child goes and with whom, put the word out to neighbors and others in the community that you would welcome information regarding any sightings of your child. Many communities have established neighborhood watch organizations. If they are watching and your child is one of the kids getting into trouble, ask them to share any information they may have.

## Set Up a Phone Tree

Some families I have worked with developed a monitoring system using a phone tree. These parents met with the parents of their child's friends and reached an agreement that when they were not sure where their child was, they would use the phone tree to locate the child or at least spread the word that the friends were out and might not be monitored.

A separate phone tree should be created for each family so that anyone is able to activate the plan should he become concerned or not know where his child has gone. The phone tree should list three names and numbers for that family to call in an emergency. Below each name should appear an additional three names and numbers that those people will call in turn. At the bottom, add a plan for occasions when a participant in the phone tree cannot be reached. You can find a blank form for constructing a phone tree at http:// www.DrPatrickMDuffy.com.

When using a phone tree, the parent calls the three people on his list, typically the parents of other children. Each of those people then calls the three on her list. As you can see, this method can be used to either seek or spread information quickly. The number of people may vary, but the more people called, the more effective the process will be. This method can also be used to provide information to other parents, such as plans to be out for the evening that would leave your home unattended and ripe for an unsupervised gathering. Those parents will then know to keep an eye on your house and to be alarmed if their child says she will be at your house and under your supervision.

# Use a Form with Location and Contact Information

Some parents have used a form to have their children provide information on where they plan to go. On this form, children provide the location where they plan to go, along with contact information and the name of the supervising adult. They are also asked to provide the time they plan to leave, the next stop if relevant, and information regarding their method of transportation and travel time between locations. You can find a blank location form at http://www .DrPatrickMDuffy.com. With this form, parents know where their child is at all times and be able to make contact. If the child does not provide the information or provides false information, she will receive punishment based on the assumption that she has gone to an unapproved location.

An important step for this approach, as well as any that rely on your child reporting information, is for you to call and verify her child's whereabouts. This can be done each time or randomly, depending on the level of concern—which should be pretty high if you're reading this book. It is also important to remember that your child answering the phone or her friend answering the phone is not sufficient to verify anything. You must speak with the supervising adult, whom you have approved.

# Wanted!

A more extreme method that some parents have utilized is the use of wanted posters. In this approach, parents create wanted posters for their child and hang them around the community. This should be done only in extreme cases, where you are unable to ascertain where your their teen goes. A wanted poster has several benefits. Obviously such a poster puts the community on alert that you are looking for your child, and it serves as an effective way of gathering information. In addition, few teens want their image, particularly an unflattering one, spread around the community with the caption "Wanted at Home by His Mommy."

## Randall

Randall was a particularly defiant child who used to stay out of the house for days at a time. He openly told his mother he was going to do as he pleased and there was nothing she could do to stop him, nearly daring her to do something to curtail his behavior. Randall's mother was particularly concerned about where he was going and the illegal activity she suspected he engaged in with a group of older peers. Her fear was that he would be hurt or arrested.

She decided that his behavior was significant enough to warrant the use of wanted posters. To make them, she found a picture of him that she knew was not his favorite and made copies of it, adding, "Wanted by His Mommy," with her phone number. She showed the poster to Randall and explained that if he stayed out again, she planned to spend the next day hanging posters throughout the community. Randall dismissed the threat, suggesting that he would take them down. However, when Randall saw the stack of copies she had made, he quickly realized that she was serious. Randall's mother never placed one poster in the community because the simple promise that she would put them up was enough to ensure that Randall came home.

The strategies you use to monitor your child will need to be tailored to what works best for you and your network of helpful people. The frequency and intensity of the monitoring effort should be sufficient to ensure that if your child is in a situation where trouble is likely, you will know about the risk and be able to respond. The specifics will vary from family to family, but to influence your child's behavior, it is essential to know where she goes, with whom she associates, and what she does.

# Exercise: Develop a Plan for Monitoring

1.  Develop a detailed weekly calendar detailing your child's activities and whereabouts by the hour (for example, "school from 7:30 until 3:00").

2.  For the times not filled by a structured activity, identify whether you are available to supervise. Consider the strategies detailed in the previous section.

3.  Identify times you are not able to effectively monitor or supervise, or when doing so will be difficult to sustain.

4.  Consider all possible resources or strategies that may be used to fill the gaps in supervision. For each period, link a possible person or strategy to the hour(s).

5.  If using additional people as support, identify the specific assistance you require (for example, phone call, being in the home) and plan how to approach them.

6.  Ensure agreement from everyone helping, and follow up afterward to make sure they will follow through as planned.

# Chapter 5

# Do Not Ignore the Relationship

By the time your child's behavior has reached a level to make you read this book, it's quite likely—and understandable—that your warm, loving feelings for him may have become hard to access. As you may remember from our discussion of parenting styles, the most effective style is that of authoritative parents. Authoritative parents establish appropriate expectations for and limits on their child's behavior, but they also show great warmth. The warmth in this relationship is essential for the behaviorally focused strategies to be effective. These approaches use the positive relationship as leverage to make them more potent. Can you imagine a stranger trying to enforce a curfew with your child? It's doubtful that this person would have much chance of being effective. And while the loving relationship may be evident for a permissive parent, another parent may find it takes some effort to bring that relationship to the fore while instituting the behavior plans.

# The Need for Warmth

Beyond making behavior plans more effective, a warm, loving relationship between parent and child serves many important functions. Demonstrated warmth provides emotional security and engenders an attachment to caregivers. As a child grows up and begins to face the big world that awaits him, he begins to be exposed to and feel the dangers that the world presents. In addition, adolescence brings many emotional pitfalls and insecurities. Warmth at home serves as a buffer against those insecurities and allows the youth to feel accepted and safe. When your child was very young, you provided protection from the monster in the closet. Now that your child is older, you provide protection from the threats of the broader world and feelings of insignificance and inadequacy. If a teen does not feel important and accepted, she may seek acceptance from other people and make bad decisions to secure their approval.

Warmth in the parent-child relationship also provides the foundation for children to develop empathy—the ability to identify with and feel the experiences of others. This relationship also provides the path through which young people learn to value interactions with other people. As you may imagine, the capacity for empathy and valuing positive interactions with others sets the tone for future relationships and for how teens interact with others. A child who does not develop empathy and does not value relationships is much more likely to struggle in relationships with peers. When young people share these relationship challenges, they tend to form a delinquent peer group. If you combine the influence of the peer group with the fact that these youths do not relate to the experiences of others or value social interaction with them, the result is that they tend to be much more willing to victimize other children or even adults. The offenses can range from minor to extreme, but our goal is to prevent any offenses whatsoever—hence the need for a warm relationship with your child.

# Effects of Your Child's Behavior

One obvious contributor to a deteriorating relationship between parent and child is the behavior of the child. It can be understandably difficult for a parent to maintain warm feelings while a teen is acting out. However, this may lead to a circular process that stalls progress. A parent feels reluctant to express warmth because of bad behavior, but that withholding of warmth contributes to difficulty altering the behavior. A parent who chooses not to allow warmth into interactions is actually contributing to the behavior that serves as a barrier to the relationship. To maintain warmth in the face of such challenging behavior, try to mentally separate the behavior from your child.

# Finding Your Warmth and Affection

You can still love your child even though you are unhappy with some of his behaviors. You may want to consider some of the things your child does that you do like—that is, catch him being good. One mother and son agreed that they wanted the warmth to return to their relationship. He agreed to choose one thing he would do for the next twenty-four hours that she would appreciate, whether it was opening the door for her or helping around the house. Her job was to identify it. At five each afternoon, she would try to guess the behavior. If she was correct, he would help her prepare dinner or some other chosen activity. If she was incorrect, he chose the activity. The result of this exercise was that he began making helpful gestures, she began paying attention to his positive traits, and regard-less of who won, they shared an activity later.

It can also help to keep in mind that your child is young and attempting to navigate her way through a big world with many influ-ences; unfortunately, some of them are influencing her in a manner that is less than helpful. It is often a good idea for parents to set aside their anger to sit down with a child and attempt to understand the situation and the influences that contributed to the behavior. I'm not asking you to excuse the behavior, but your frustration may decrease if you understand why it occurs. Furthermore, this is a very different conversation from what your child may be used to, and he may appreciate simply being able to talk and have you understand. Keep in mind that you can express your understanding of what the situation is like from your child's perspective without accepting or excusing the behavior.

I have worked with some families that found it helpful to look through an old photo album and remind themselves of good times with their children. This can be done among adults but can also be effective if the whole family participates. Parents might get out the album after dinner or while the family is watching television and casually show a picture or ask the child if she remembers something from the past. Many teens enjoy that activity and will willingly sit with a parent and laugh about old stories recalled by the pictures.

A glance through a photo album may spark thoughts of an activ-ity that you and your child used to do together. This can be a great way to introduce the idea of an outing together. Some parents simply offer to take a child on an outing of her choice—with an obvious need for some limits. Joint activities show an interest in your child and what she enjoys. It's also another deposit in the bank of warm memories and sentiments, which might be a little depleted at the moment.

Many families have songs they used to sing or games they used to play together. If it's done without fanfare, kids may go along with the activity and actually enjoy it. I would suggest not making it appear to be an intervention, and not doing it when your child is preparing to go out with friends. Rather, during a time when the child is home, casually look at a photo album and point out a picture or casually start singing songs and playfully encourage her participation. If she chooses not to engage, don't feel defeated. The goal is to generate feelings of warmth in you; your child's participation is a nice bonus, but not essential.

# Exercise: Build Warm Feelings

1. Consider the things that make you nostalgic (songs, photos, places).

2. Identify a time to spend an hour enjoying those things several times during the week.

3. Ask your child to participate if you wish.

4. Spend time thinking about happy moments and identify things about your child that remind you of him at a younger age.

5. Consider things your child does now that make you happy or proud, and plan how and when to tell him how much you appreciate those things.

6. When there is peace in the house, share your warm thoughts with your child. You may follow this with an invitation to a shared activity (for example, going to a movie, a fishing trip).

7. During the activity, do not spend time discussing the problematic behavior; just enjoy the event.

8. Follow up later by sharing how much you appreciate spending time with him even if there are times you argue.

# Conflict from Setting Expectations

A second obvious barrier to remembering that warm relationship with your child is open conflict. Obviously, it is quite difficult to bring loving feelings to the surface in the midst of an open argument. Many of these conflicts arise in the context of a parent enforcing a rule or setting an expectation. In chapter 3, I asked that you not argue with your child. You're less likely to have an extended argument if you simply tell your teen that she broke the rule and will receive the consequence. Each additional sentence provides another possible topic for debate. After allowing some time for the situation to settle, you may explain to your child that you love her and are not going to allow her to behave in such a manner. Some teens will respond by arguing, in which case you simply leave the room, but some youths will accept your explanation and their punishment. This strategy is usually effective, but there are certainly situations that require more attention and effort to avoid conflict. Those strategies will be discussed in chapter 6.

# I Just Don't Have Time

Parents often explain that one difficulty they face in creating an atmosphere of warmth is that they lack the time. Many parents have job responsibilities that require a great deal of their time. They may be providing for the needs of other children or elderly family members. They may have other responsibilities beyond the home and their job. I can certainly understand that finding the time to recreate feelings of warmth can be difficult, particularly when you factor in the time you may already be spending on school meetings and trying to track where your child has gone and with whom. I understand this is not easy, and I do not want to minimize the effect it has on your life. Having said that, I suggest you prioritize finding time to reacquaint yourself with your love for your child. Would you be willing to skip your favorite television show for an evening? Would you be willing to skip reading the newspaper on Saturday or Sunday morning? Is there someone who could help with some of your other duties to create time for you to engage in such an important pursuit?

I understand that your relationship with your teen may be strained at the moment, but remember that you are making the effort to read this book out of love and concern. While it is understandable, and necessary, that you express disapproval for inappropriate behavior, it is also important that you remember your love for your child and express it when possible. This is important for him developmentally, important for your effort to bring his behavior under control, and important for you.

# Chapter 6

# Managing Conflict

I have said before that I don't want you to engage in conflict with your child. I do not mean that you should give in to your child's desires so as to avoid conflict; instead, consider your authority as absolute and without need for justification or debate. Simply state your decision to your child and leave the room if necessary. However, this may be overly simplistic in some situations. In this chapter I discuss family conflict and some strategies to help you avoid or defuse it without giving in to your teen's demands. There will also be a discussion of planning for safety, for situations that warrant such planning. The lessons discussed in this chapter will be relevant for any conflict in the home, whether between siblings, between parents and children, or between spouses.

I want to be clear that if there is violence in your home, you should be working with a licensed therapist, preferably a therapist from an evidence-based program, to help reduce the conflict and make your home safe. The strategies outlined in this book can be effective, but it is difficult to employ them objectively if you are involved in such situations. You may be able to apply these lessons to avoid verbal confrontations, but if there is risk of physical harm, seek professional intervention; and call 911 in case of imminent physical conflict. In seeking help from professionals, make sure they are working with you on strategies like those outlined in this chapter. If they spend time exploring your childhood or existential concerns, seek someone else. Those approaches may make you feel better about yourself, but the good feeling is unlikely to last long if you have a violent confrontation with your child, or anyone else, that night.

# Secure Weapons If Necessary

Seriously consider the risk of physical harm that exists in your home. If there is a history of violence involving weapons, secure any objects that have been or could be used as a weapon. Comb the house for traditional weapons as well as household items that could be used as such, including tools, heavy blunt objects like some lamps, and base-ball bats. The kind of search you do depends on the level of risk. When evaluating risk, please keep in mind that your new disciplinary strategies will increase pressure on your child as well as you, your spouse, and anyone else involved. The increased pressure may elevate the risk. If you have any reason to think that an object could be used to hurt someone, it is crucial that you secure the object before it can be used for harm. If you find that you locked something away unnecessarily, you can feel good that the risk was not as high as you thought. People frequently ask how far parents should go in securing possible weapons. The answer depends on the circumstances and the people involved. I worked with one family who ate from paper plates and used plastic knives and forks for three weeks. Was it over-kill? I don't know, but I do know that the child didn't pick up any kitchen utensils in a fit of rage. Once any potential weapons are secured, you can work to minimize the conflicts that make such items dangerous.

# **Exercise:** Plan to Secure Weapons

1.  *Identify the current level of risk of physical confrontation in your home. Now, imagine the current conflict intensified.*

2.  *If such prediction allows for even a remote possibility of using an object in a physical confrontation, identify any objects that might be used.*

3.  *Plan where you will keep those objects out of reach.*

# Recognize the Patterns

If you review the last few arguments or outbursts that have occurred in your home, it may not shock you that familial conflict tends to follow predictable sequences. The specific content or subject matter may change, but the behavior patterns tend to repeat. How many times have you been on the verge of an argument with your child and thought, "Here we go again"? You probably have a similar thought if you argue frequently with your spouse or when you hear the interaction among siblings begin to escalate. There is something familiar to you about the interaction. At that moment, you have recognized the pattern of escalation. This recognition of patterns and sequences will be an important element in minimizing conflict in the home.

A typical parent-child conflict may progress much like the one described in the figure that follows, figure 3.

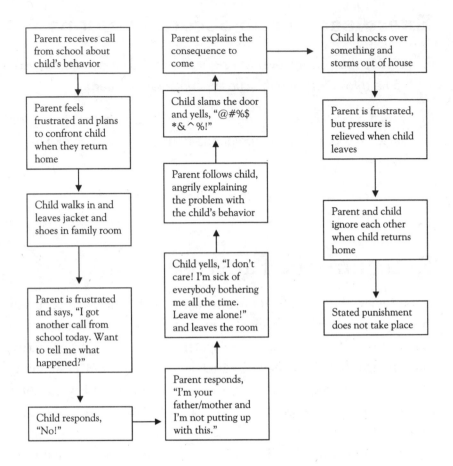

Figure 3

# Prediction and Avoidance

To reduce conflict in the home, it is helpful to be able to predict it and to notice when strong emotions begin to arise. Once emotions kick in, it is difficult to do anything other than follow the pattern. And it is extremely difficult to set emotion aside and carefully consider a response when confronted by an angry outburst. In the scenario described in figure 3, the parent probably felt a surge of anger and adrenaline at the point when the child responded, "No!" to the parent's request for information. The parent most likely became embroiled in an angry exchange before recognizing the familiar pattern.

Based on previous behavior, we could probably predict that the parent and child would find themselves in such a conflict when the parent confronted the child regarding the behavior at school. If the parent had recognized that the sequence actually began with the phone call from the school, she could have predicted what would follow. This ability to predict makes it possible to plan the approach to the situation, recognize the early stages, and steer the sequence to a different end.

# Deborah

Deborah worked long hours at her job. Her children typically came home from school, made a mess in the kitchen, and then made an equal mess in the living room. The children also engaged in challenging behavior that led to many notes from school and calls from concerned neighbors. The typical pattern was that Deborah would come home physically exhausted and be confronted by the mess in the house, complaints from neighbors or school, and complaints from one sibling about another. Deborah would feel overwhelmed and frustrated, and she would start yelling at the kids. They would respond, depending on their role in the trouble of the day, and the house was soon awash in arguing and yelling. Just as in figure 3, Deborah found herself in a predictable pattern, and once we recognized it, we were able to use our ability to predict patterns to develop a more effective strategy. We recognized that Deborah could use her commute time to prepare for what she would face upon her return home. She placed a reminder on the visor of her car that prompted her to prepare herself for her arrival and to follow the agreed-upon plan. Deborah rehearsed the plan in her mind, and when she entered the home, she simply repeated to her children that she did not want to deal with them at the moment, and that she was going to take a shower. Deborah saw the daily mess in the house on her way to the bathroom, and she used the time in the shower to relax, clear her mind, and plan for when she returned downstairs. The ultimate goal, of course, was for Deborah to get her children's behavior under control so she would no longer be confronted with the same scenario, but first we needed to reduce conflict so that Deborah could utilize a more effective approach.

## Reduce the Influence of Friends

Once you know how arguments arise, you can plan to hold conversations in a more favorable setting. For example, there may be particular people who add to the probability of conflict. Friends of teens commonly serve as such an influence. When confronted in front of peers, teens may become argumentative to boost their image. This behavior is commonly met with laughter from the peers, and their telling the story to others also brings laughter and status. Knowing that their presence is likely to contribute to an argument, parents can ask their child's friends to leave before having a discussion that could end in argument. Depending on the urgency, they might also choose to simply wait until the friends are not present.

## Identify People Who Reduce Conflict

Another way to decrease the probability of conflict is to consider whether there are people whose presence makes conflict less likely.

Some children are quite happy to argue with a parent but will not raise their voices in the presence of another parent, a grandparent, an uncle, or a respected neighbor. If there are such people in your child's life, you may consider having a potentially inflammatory exchange only when these people are present, or you may request that they be present at an appointed time. If your plan involves others, it is important that they understand specifically what you want them to do and that they agree. For example, someone who has a strong relationship with your teen may be able to take him to another room and encourage him to handle the situation calmly and not make it worse. She may also be able to give a signal that the conversation has become too emotional and send everyone to different rooms. I have seen cases where a person came over to help, but the situation deteriorated quickly because it was unclear what was being asked of him and so his response added to the conflict.

## Address Any Medical Needs

Some psychiatric conditions may contribute to a tendency to become emotional or aggressive. If there is someone in the home who has such a condition, or whom you suspect may have one, it is important to ensure that any medical needs are addressed. The effects of some conditions may persist despite medication and contribute to arguments. In such situations, you should learn to recognize the signs, just as you factor signs of anger into your planning. You may need psychiatric assistance to adjust medications, or you may simply need to plan potentially volatile discussions for a time when that person is not present. If neither is possible, note any signs of increased agitation and factor those into your strategy. You may also consult with a physician for advice on how to help calm the emotions associated with the particular diagnosis.

# Factor in Substance Abuse

Substance abuse is a predictable contributor to conflict. As such, it may be wise to plan to have difficult interactions at a time participants are not impaired.

## Richard

Richard and his mother, Sandy, frequently engaged in violent conflict. Examination of their fighting revealed a common sequence of events. Richard had a curfew of eleven on weekends. Sandy wanted him to be home on time because she frequently worked in the morning; he also had a pattern of getting into trouble late at night. Not surprisingly, Richard was not fond of his curfew and rarely complied, which angered Sandy. A typical Friday night would find Sandy watching the clock, her anxiety and anger building as eleven o'clock approached. At the specified time, Richard was often not home, and Sandy would sit in the living room smoking cigarettes, staring at the door, and becoming angrier with each tick of the clock. Richard typically returned home closer to one than to his specified curfew. In addition to being late, he was likely to be intoxicated. The combination of his intoxication and Sandy's mounting anger created a combustible environment that often exploded when he entered the home. Sandy would yell at him for being late and proclaim that he would not be able to go out for some time. In his impaired state, Richard responded with aggressive language, and the argument often ended in violence.

Richard and Sandy were following a predictable pattern, but it could be altered by changing the circumstances. We did not want Sandy to ignore the curfew violation, but neither did we want violence. To alter the pattern, we agreed that at eleven o'clock, if Richard had not returned home, Sandy would go to her bedroom, where she would watch television, read, or listen to music to minimize her emotional reaction. She would stay awake until Richard came home, to verify that he got home safely, and she would note his time of arrival. Instead of having the conflict while she was seething and Richard was intoxicated, Sandy would then go to bed. When she woke up in the morning, Sandy would get dressed, go into Richard's room, and wake him up to explain that he had missed curfew and would receive the stated consequence. At this point, she would leave the room, and if she had to go to work, she would do so. Under this system, Sandy had the evening to sleep and let go of her emotions. In addition, in the morning Richard was sleepy and felt less like fighting. By changing the sequence of their interactions, we were able to dramatically alter the result. Simply going to her room allowed Sandy the space and distance to suspend the interaction until the following morning, when conditions no longer supported physical confrontation.

# Exercise: Develop a Plan to Avoid Conflict

1. *Carefully consider the last conflict you had with your child. Beginning from the moment you identified it as significant, think backward to what happened just before that, and before that, until you have identified who said and did what and the various influences that maintained the conflict.*

2.  *Consider topics likely to prompt conflict and the people who should, or should not, be there the next time you address this topic.*

3.  *Develop a plan for how you will deliver the required message and avoid the conflict, either with the help of others or by removing yourself from the situation.*

4.  *If others are involved in the plan, contact them and secure their agreement.*

5.  *Practice the plan, and identify any changes that need to be made.*

# Set the Goal of Reduced Fighting

At a time when nobody is angry, you and your family should recognize that nobody wants to have high levels of conflict and agree that you will work to decrease the battles. You may introduce the topic by simply explaining that you love everyone in your family and you would like to work together to stop the fighting. Make it clear that this is not the time to blame anyone or attack each other. This is about working together; if the tone becomes aggressive, stop the conversation. If there are sensitivities from previous incidents or hurt feelings, speak with the people who have them individually. Sometimes conflict actually serves to undermine parents' efforts at discipline. If that is the case in your home, your child may have some incentive to maintain conflict. If she is not willing to commit to turning down the volume in your home, simply explain that you love her and do not want to fight, so you plan to take steps to prevent the intense arguments of the past. Ideally the whole family will share the goal of reducing arguments, but if they do not, those who do agree may still make plans to remove themselves from the conflict.

# Early Recognition

Conflicts may arise that we cannot avoid. When arguments start, parents often find themselves engaged before they realize what is happening. In these instances, the earlier you recognize the signs of escalation, the more successful you are likely to be in steering the discussion to a different ending.

## Identify Signs That You're Getting Angry

To learn to recognize signs of escalation, we need to carefully consider how each person typically reacts. Let's start with you. Think about a couple of recent instances when you were angry. How can you tell you're starting to get angry? Certain thoughts may enter your mind. A more detailed sequence from figure 3 might include the mother thinking that she is "not going to let him be disrespectful and get away with it." The mother may identify this as an early warning sign. What do you do and what do you feel? Typically, people feel their heart rate begin to accelerate. You may feel an adrenaline rush and notice a difference in your breathing. Many people begin to feel warm or feel a lump in the throat. Do you begin to yell or have difficulty forming sentences? Some people begin to move faster as they get angry and find it difficult to perform activities that require concentration and fine motor skills. Whatever cues you observe, it's important that you begin to identify signs of agitation and that you attend to them when they occur.

If your child has agreed to work on decreasing conflict, you may ask her how she knows when you are starting to get angry. She has certainly seen you get angry and may be able to describe the pattern more accurately than you can. This may be helpful for you and may also allow her to interrupt the sequence if she sees it developing.

Also ask your spouse or significant other. Each person may notice different clues. If you fail to predict and avoid a conflict, catching these warning signs may be your last chance to remove yourself before the interaction becomes too heated.

# How to Tell When Your Significant Other Is Angry

Now consider your spouse or significant other. What are the signs that tell you he is getting angry? Does he become loud or silent? Does he begin to yell or flail his arms as he speaks? Many people have facial expressions or movements that indicate displeasure. Some people literally turn red when they become angry. (I have yet to see someone whose ears actually produce steam, though.) Does your significant other move closer to the target of his anger? I have listed some common indicators; now try to visualize how your significant other looks, sounds, and behaves when he becomes angry. Here again, you may want to ask your child what indicators she notices. You may also encourage your significant other to consider his own responses and how he recognizes that he is becoming angry.

# Signs Your Child Is Getting Angry

Go through these same steps for your child and anyone else who is likely to be involved in the conflict. This may seem like a difficult exercise, but I have seen families get a big kick out of pointing out each other's patterns. In addition to generating some laughter, this can be extremely helpful in your efforts to minimize conflict.

# Establish a Signal

With the goal of reducing the frequency and intensity of fighting, it can be helpful to establish a signal that you are following the familiar path of conflict. The reason for a signal rather than a phrase is that many people do not really hear what the other person is saying during a conflict. You can choose any signal, as long as everyone agrees and it will not be seen as disrespectful or contribute to the conflict. I recognize that this caveat may rule out some signals currently exchanged in your family, but there are many others that meet the criteria. Many families use the time-out signal used in sports; some tug on an ear. No matter what signal you choose, everyone should agree that when the signal is given, they will stop talking immediately and not try to get in one last point or barb. They must not question the signal. When the signal is given, the participants in the conflict should separate and go to previously identified neutral corners. If someone does not agree to leave the room, you should still leave the scene. The time apart will allow everyone to cool down and help to defuse the situation.

Once everyone has retreated to neutral corners, they should engage in activities that take their minds off the current conflict. This must not involve alcohol, other drugs, or property destruction. Some people prefer to take a bath; some relax by reading, listening to music, or engaging in exercise. Everyone should engage in their chosen activities for a specified time sufficient to calm the emotions and stop the argument.

# **Exercise:** Engage the Family to Avoid Fighting

1. *Develop a plan for how you will call the family together to explain that you love them and do not want to have arguing and fight-*

*ing in the family. Plan to explain that you hope to avoid fights by recognizing the signs early and stopping the fight.*

2.  *During a time free of conflict, gather the willing participants and offer your plan.*

3.  *Once in agreement, everyone should describe how they know when they are getting angry (talking only about themselves), and listen while others describe what they see when that person becomes angry. Playful demonstration is acceptable, but avoid blame and ridicule.*

4.  *The family should examine a common sequence to identify points where a different response might avoid escalation. Avoid getting into another argument over this, focusing rather on the broader sequence.*

5.  *The family should then agree on a sign that will be acceptable to all involved that warning signs have been noticed and "combatants" should disperse.*

6.  *Identify where each person will go during the time-out and when it will be acceptable to reconvene.*

# Uh-Oh! It's Happening!

Despite your best efforts, there may be times when a conflict occurs that you did not predict—when you either missed the early warning signs, or noticed them when you were already so angry that you disregarded them to make your point. In those instances, try to explain that you need to leave the room and take a time-out. If others are arguing, you may suggest that everyone separate, or else ask the most amenable to leave the room with you and try to calm the battling parties. Explain that you understand they are angry and you want to hear what they have to say, but right now the yelling is too much. You may encourage those people to take a walk, listen to music, or do anything that helps them relax.

# Physical Violence

For some families, their typical sequence may potentially lead to a violent conflict. I hope this does not describe you, but some families become so embroiled in conflict that the end result is violence. This may come in the form of physical attacks or property destruction. In those cases, families should not allow the conflict to run its natural course. Those families need to have a plan for getting out of the situation before someone gets hurt or something gets broken. It is also advisable to seek the help of a professional.

## Signs That Violence Is Coming

To determine when violence is imminent, examine the indicators much as you did in the last exercise, paying particular attention to anyone likely to initiate violence. This may be a sensitive topic; do not force others to join the conversation if they are uncomfortable or if it's likely to spark an argument. People who have been victims of violence or who fear it may not want to be part of this conversation. Likewise, people who become violent may not want to be involved because they may feel accused or the violence may actually get them what they want. If family members are not willing to participate, go through the process on your own; this is valuable in promoting safety.

## Get Out!

If you notice that you, your spouse, your child, or anyone else is beginning to show signs of resorting to physical violence, you, and others at risk, should get out immediately and call for help if necessary. When safety is at stake, there is no need to give a signal; that opportunity has been missed. At this point, your primary goal is safety. Get to a safe place. Depending on the situation, this may mean a different room, outside, the neighbors' house, or any place you identify. Wait for help to arrive or for the situation to subside.

## **Exercise:** Make an Escape Plan

1. *As in the previous exercise, family members should take turns identifying signs that violence is imminent. This includes self-assessment and feedback from other members of the family.*

2. *Have members of the family detail an escape plan, including when to leave, where to go, and whom to call (neighbors, family, police) and what response you would like from them.*

3. *You should also consider, based on the typical duration of the episode, how long to remain away from the potentially violent person before returning. Sometimes it is possible to enlist someone with a good relationship with the perpetrator to assess the risk or help calm the situation.*

4. *If other people are to be used as resources, include them in the plan, to ensure their agreement. The plan should also include what to do if those people are not available.*

# The Aftermath

Once the intensity of the conflict has decreased to a normal level, it will be helpful to resolve the issue if this can be done safely. If you were attempting to give your child a consequence, you should return to explain that you know he does not like it, but he broke the rule and will receive the consequence. You may also add that he has earned an additional consequence for aggressive behavior. If you started the conflict by denying a request, simply explain that you understand he would like whatever the request was, but it will not be granted. If two siblings were fighting, you may need to give each a consequence. If you were the one who was close to becoming violent, it would be advisable to model good behavior: say you needed to leave the room because you do not want to have fights any longer, then reiterate your decision. After giving your final decision, leave the room. Beware of sparking another strong reaction, and continue to look for warning signs, being ready to leave the area if indicated. Try to avoid the typical pattern of conflict and not allow escalation to make you give in to any demands.

# Practice Makes Perfect

As emotion and anxiety rise in an argument, the ability to carefully plan each response is diminished, and the behavior that comes most naturally is likely to surface. For the new strategy to win out, you and your family should practice walking through scenarios where each person gives an atypical response. Include anyone you are asking to be present as a part of the effort; it is important that they too understand and be prepared. And, for this to be effective, you should make this practice as realistic as possible. Think of how the military trains soldiers by drilling desired behavior under fire. To increase the likelihood that soldiers will perform well in battle, they are put through repeated drills under simulated battle circumstances. I hope the conflict in your home is not as serious as military battle, but one can always learn from what others do.

# **Exercise:** Practice Your Plan

1. *During a peaceful time, explain to your family that you would like to practice a plan to avoid fighting. If anyone does not wish to participate, gently encourage him or her. If some decide not to participate, continue without them. Assign parts and role-play a typical scenario. Switching roles can make it more comfortable and fun while allowing people to demonstrate the anger signs of other participants. Again, playfulness is acceptable, but blame and ridicule are to be avoided.*

2. *If possible, include people whose presence you would request in an actual argument.*

3. *Practice scenarios as they tend to develop, but employ the new strategies at the appropriate point.*

4. *Realistic role-play is helpful but should not be used to rehash current disagreements; everyone is on the same team in this exercise as they work to avoid conflict.*

5. *As you practice, note strategies that seem helpful and change any that may not work.*

# Document the Plan

In addition to practicing the plan, it can be helpful to write it down. Some families choose to give everyone a copy; others post it somewhere in the house. The process of writing it down formalizes it as a procedure to follow. It also allows you to review it before beginning a potentially volatile conversation or to reference it once the conversation has started. When the plan is written, you can review it frequently so you are more likely to put the plan into action when necessary. The format you use to create your plan is completely up to you. You should use what is easy and workable for you. There are a variety of elements that may be helpful to document, including prevention plans, early warning signs, later warning signs, and signs of imminent violence, as well as steps to take at each stage. I have included some examples and formats for your consideration at http://www.DrPatrickMDuffy.com.

# What Worked, and What Didn't?

Once you have created a plan and used it, look back and closely examine the sequence of events. Carefully consider what took place. Are there points where you were able to identify patterns, where you were able to act differently or encourage different behavior than typically occurs? Congratulate anyone who did something atypical. This is a huge step toward decreasing conflict. You may have successfully done some things differently but ended up falling back into the old pattern. You may have attempted to do something different, but someone else responded in a way that was not expected, which led to conflict. In such situations, examine where efforts broke down and how the conflict evolved. Consider how the plan needs to be changed or how people need to respond differently given this new information. Work continuously to perfect the plan and make it more effective while not losing sight of the advances you have made. It may take some time to rid your home of conflict.

## Eric and Cindy

Eric and his mother, Cindy, typically engaged in heated verbal exchanges. These exchanges seemed to happen whenever Cindy attempted to give a consequence or refused to grant a request. Cindy's husband was frequently away for work, and she did not have many other people in her life on whom she could call for help. On top of being emotionally exhausting for Cindy, the aggressive exchanges decreased her ability to effectively set limits with Eric, because she became so frustrated that she would give in to his demands. One day, Cindy explained to Eric that she planned to continue to enforce the rules of the house, but she was going to make an effort to avoid fighting with him because she loved him and did not like to fight. She suggested that when they noticed a conversation becoming argumentative, they should both exit the room and calm themselves. Predictably, they had an argument the next day after school when Eric refused to do his chores or homework, thus prompting Cindy to set a limit. Cindy did an excellent job of identifying the sequence and explained that she was going to her room to calm down and would address the situation later. When Cindy went to her room, Eric followed and began beating on the door and yelling through the door. Ultimately, Cindy returned to the normal pattern.

The following day, Cindy and I examined the sequence of the argument. I praised Cindy for her new ability to identify the sequence of their arguments and to remove herself from the situation. Though they ended up fighting nonetheless, these new behaviors were huge advances in her effort to avoid engaging in fights with her son. After considering the sequence, we realized that the plan had not been successful because we had not predicted that Eric would follow her and overwhelm her ability to remain uninvolved. We decided to build on Cindy's success but alter the plan. We also planned to provide an additional consequence for Eric's verbal aggression in the future but decided not to introduce it until we had stopped the conflict. The new plan was for Cindy to identify the conflict and state that she was leaving the room, but this time she would get in her car and ride around the block listening to music.

A couple of days later, Eric and Cindy became involved in another conflict. Once again, Cindy was able to successfully identify the pattern and remove herself from the room. She walked out the front door and got in the car as planned. As she started the car, Eric jumped in the passenger seat and began to verbally abuse her. Cindy was not sure what to do, and they found themselves back in the familiar fight.

Cindy understood that she was on the right track and felt good about her ability to remove herself from the situation. Upon careful consideration, we decided using the car was still a good idea. We created a contingency plan in case Eric followed her to the car the next time. As you might expect, the pattern surfaced again a few days later. Cindy explained that she was going to leave. Eric quickly ran to get in the car to prevent Cindy from escaping the conflict, which Eric had learned worked to his advantage.

Cindy got in the car and drove away with Eric in the passenger seat berating her. This time Cindy drove to the police station and got the attention of some officers. She introduced them to Eric and explained that she was trying to get Eric's behavior under control, then asked them to let her know if they saw Eric in the community or heard of him doing anything wrong. After talking with the police, Cindy and Eric returned home, where Cindy provided the consequence for the original behavior. She now had an effective plan for removing herself from the conflict, since Eric did not like the idea of returning to the police station. An added benefit was that Cindy now had police officers assisting her in monitoring the community for signs of Eric behaving inappropriately or associating with delinquent youths. They understood what Cindy was trying to accomplish and were willing to help.

The case of Eric and Cindy is a great example of carefully considering what went well with a plan to avoid conflict and also where the plan failed. In each instance, we tried to build on parts of the plan that had gone well while adjusting for Eric's response. Success did not come immediately, but Cindy was eventually able to avoid the conflict and give Eric both a consequence for his behavior and an increased consequence for his verbal aggression. Over time, the verbal aggression waned, and Cindy was able to consistently provide limits and to offer reinforcement for appropriate behavior, such as not resorting to verbal aggression. As the behavior diminished, the relationship between mother and son became much more peaceful.

One of the most satisfying measures of progress for families in treatment is a reduction in conflict in the home. This change makes the rest of the effort more tolerable and more likely to be effective. Though reducing conflict is not easy, it can be accomplished by carefully studying how conflict occurs, planning new strategies, practicing, and continuously evaluating the effort. If you do this carefully and sincerely, the ensuing reduction in conflict will be quite rewarding for you and your family.

## Common Parental Concerns

### I don't think we really need to do that much planning.

You may not need this much planning, and I hope you do not. However, if there is a chance, based on past interactions in your family, that violence may occur, you should absolutely plan and practice (with the guidance of a professional). The level of planning should be based on the risk. Do you simply need to avoid an argument, or do you need to plan for leaving the home? Either way, you should plan and practice. Think about it as insurance. Your home may not burn down, you may not have a catastrophic injury, and you may not total your car, but insurance is still a good idea to avoid the consequences of not being prepared if such events do occur.

### It's easier to just give my child what she wants.

It is—for the moment—but giving a child what she wants in response to conflict increases the likelihood of such behavior in the future. If you give your dog a treat when you tell him to sit, he is more likely to sit the next time. If you give your dog a treat when he lunges aggressively at another dog, he is more likely to lunge the next time. When you give in, you are teaching your child that an aggressive outburst is effective and achieves her goal. In addition, it keeps you in a position of never being in control in the house, and contributes to sustaining the concerning behavior. This is not a simple question of whether or not to give in and stop the conflict, because the two do not have equal outcomes down the road. When you consider your long-term goals for your child compared with your current fears, it is clear that a few repetitions of an escape plan are well worth the effort if they allow you to effectively enforce limits in the home.

# Chapter 7

# Build Your Team

Reversing a pattern of delinquent behavior takes significant effort, planning, time, and emotional energy. I do not want you to undertake this process completely on your own. My hope is that you and others, whether relatives, friends, neighbors, members of your church, or anyone else with whom you have a relationship, will work together to significantly change the conditions in your child's life that allow the troublesome behaviors to continue. This requires careful consideration of your need for support, potential support people, and what those support people can do to help you along this journey.

## Assessing Your Support Needs

The first step in enlisting support is to identify the type of support you need. Some parents need substantial support in fulfilling concrete tasks or responsibilities. If you are a parent with two jobs, monitoring your child after school may be difficult without assistance. If you plan to have your child participate in activities after school, you may require help with transportation or child care for your other children so that you can work with this child. Some families may require financial assistance to pay registration fees or to purchase necessary equipment or clothing.

# People to Help with Tasks

Start by evaluating your current resources. Consider the people in your life whom you consider supportive, as well as those you have not previously considered. If your car broke down tomorrow morning and you needed a ride to work, whom would you call? If you needed to run an errand or take one of your children to the doctor, whom would you ask to watch the others? Consider people whom you may have recently asked for assistance or people who might have helped if asked. You may also want to consider people who have asked you for assistance. I don't mean to suggest they owe you, but their request indicates that they believe your relationship is close enough that you can ask them to reciprocate.

# Emotional Support

We all have tough days; you certainly do if you have chosen to read this far. We also have occasions when we have accomplished something and look forward to sharing the news with someone. As you embark on this journey to change the behavior of your child, you will have tough days, and I sincerely hope that you will also have many successes to share with others. We all feel a need for emotional support in both good times and hard times. It will be important to you on this journey.

Just as you assessed your resources for assistance with concrete tasks, evaluate the people in your life, identifying those you currently rely on for emotional needs. Think about people you call or visit when you have had a bad day. For some, this may be a spouse; for others, it is a friend. It may be a combination of people; there is no need to limit yourself to just one person. In addition to those who provide a shoulder to cry on, take a moment to identify the people you call when things have gone well. Do you ask friends to go out to dinner or for a drink? There may be many people with whom you share emotional information and experiences, and those people will be important to you in this process. It's quite likely that several have been helpful as you coped with your child's behavior to this point.

## Constructive Criticism

Though emotional support is crucial, you also need a person, or several people, who will provide an honest evaluation of your effort. These are people who provide encouragement in the face of difficulty and reassure you that you are headed in the right direction. They should also be people willing to tell you when your effort is less than helpful, or when you are working against your long-term goals. For example, you may find yourself in a heated argument with your child that leads to you giving in and allowing him to go to a party you had opposed. You may tell a friend, who sympathizes with you and validates your feelings of hurt and despair. This is an important form of support. However, it is also important to have someone who points out to you that though you ended the conflict, you have allowed, enabled, and reinforced your child's defiance. This person may walk through the situation with you and consider possible strategies that might have led to a different outcome, or she may point out barriers that kept you from using the strategies you had considered. She may offer to be on location the next time or to provide encouragement by phone to help you stick with your plan and enforce your limits.

As you consider the supports in your life, you may identify people who fill various roles. Typically some people provide certain types of support and others provide different ones. You may notice an abundance of some types of support but have fewer resources elsewhere. Most likely there is no one person who provides all kinds of support, with the possible exception of a spouse or significant other. There is no magic number of people that you should have. The goal is to have people available to meet whatever needs you may have now and in the future. This committee can be large or small, as long as they meet your needs.

# Where to Look for Additional Support

You may find that you need to build additional support. When considering potential helpers, it is helpful to consider people with whom you have a personal relationship or the framework from which to build a personal relationship. These may include neighbors or people in extended family. Also consider seeking support from a colleague at work or from members of your church congregation.

## Common Parental Concerns

**Why are you suggesting that I seek assistance through personal relationships versus social services or "the system"?**

This is a common question. The support you will need, whether it involves monitoring your child after school or being present to help avoid conflict, does not fit into the nine-to-five availability of most professionals, and they cannot come to your home on short notice. Professionals do not have the same access or influence in the family as those with personal relationships, and are thus unable to be as intense in their effort or as effective in the long term. In addition, when your case is closed, that professional will no longer be available. If you need assistance monitoring your child on the weekend because of your work schedule, you will continue to need that assistance beyond the bounds of the case. A neighbor or relative is more likely to be available when you need him and for as long as you need him.

**I don't want to let everyone know about my family's problems.**

They already know. If your child's behavior is bad enough to make you read this book, then your neighbors are probably aware, your family is most likely aware, and so are other members of the community. Would you rather have them see the behavior continue, or would you prefer they know that you are working to get the behavior under control?

Even if others were not aware of the troublesome behavior, is your desire to avoid embarrassment important enough that you would rather hide the facts than change your child's behavior? If your child is engaged in serious misbehavior, would you not endure this embarrassment if you knew it would prevent the consequences this behavior may lead to in the future?

You may also want to consider reaching out to new people. The manager of a store or community center may be an excellent resource, though he may not be able to provide emotional support or evaluate and encourage your efforts. If you have few social outlets or relationships on which to draw, consider developing such relationships. You may find support by participating in activities you enjoy. Carefully consider your typical day: are there people you see frequently who may be potential social connections for you?

## Sarah

Sarah had done tremendous work on enforcing limits in the home and had some success, but we noticed that she was beginning to waver in her commitment. She explained that the work she was doing, in addition to her job, was taking a toll on her, and she was having a difficult time remaining energetic due to the level of emotional involvement required. We decided that Sarah needed some outlets to express her frustrations. The problem was that Sarah did not have many friends; nor did she have an abundance of time. We asked her to carefully consider a typical week and to list people she spoke to on the phone, in her neighborhood, at work, in church, and so on. We identified a group of women in Sarah's neighborhood who walked together each morning. Sarah frequently saw them walking past her house, and they exchanged greetings. We worked with Sarah to help her formally introduce herself to them and see if it would be okay for her to join their group. Notice that I did not tell Sarah to ask the women to help with her child's behavior. She simply asked to join a group of nice ladies walking around the neighborhood. They agreed. Given that these walks occurred daily, it did not take long before the women began to ask about her family. Sarah revealed more information as she became comfortable, and her level of comfort increased as her friendship with these women developed.

## Pamela

Pamela was in a similar situation, with few contacts in the neighborhood, so we asked if there were any people at work with whom she typically interacted but whom she had not considered. Pamela explained that she was a driver for a company and spent most of her day alone. With that in mind, we carefully analyzed her week, looking for anyone who could help. There was another driver she frequently saw at the coffee machine in the morning. This may not seem like the foundation for a deep relationship, but Pamela considered the gentleman a very nice guy. We created a plan for Pamela to greet the other driver and start a conversation. For a couple of days, Pamela simply smiled and greeted the man. After that, she began to ask questions about his route, and eventually about events of the day, such as, "Did you get caught in that traffic from the accident on the interstate yesterday?" They began to share tales of their routes and people they encountered. Over time, they developed a rapport and the other driver became someone with whom Pamela could share her accomplishments and struggles.

## Common Parental Concerns

### Doesn't this seem conniving?

Making friends? If you were simply trying to manipulate someone into doing something for you, then yes, it would be conniving. However, I am talking about a person with few social outlets trying to develop friendships with people. Social outlets are good for people for many reasons, beyond simply serving as a way to express your concerns about your day. People frequently seek to make friends after they have moved to new areas because friendships are important. To seek genuine friendships when there is a need is more like seeking friends after a move than manipulation.

# Match the Support to the Need

Once you have identified some people who could potentially help support you, carefully consider the type of support you need. By this I mean that you should consider specifically what you would like a support person to do. Once you have defined the need, it becomes much easier to identify who might be able to help. Everyone has things they do well and things they do not do well, as well as differing schedules and activities.

In your consideration of people who may be helpful, I encourage you not to exclude anyone based upon criteria that may not be relevant. Having weaknesses does not mean that a person is unable to help, nor does it mean that the person is unwilling to make an effort out of concern for you or your child.

# Nancy and Paul

Nancy and Paul both worked early shifts and were having trouble getting their daughter to attend school. To make matters worse, they left for work at the time their daughter needed to wake up for school. Nancy woke her daughter each morning before she left but could not ensure that she followed through with getting dressed and going to school. We decided that it would be helpful for Nancy and Paul to find someone to check on their daughter and make sure she got to school. We created a list of people who might be available and willing. Nancy had mentioned a cousin who lived a few blocks from them, but she thought he would not be able to help because he was a heavy drinker, though she loved him and had a good relationship with him.

Their initial reaction was to rule him out, but we decided to inquire further. It turned out that he typically started drinking in the afternoon and continued until he went to bed. Though he did frequently drink to excess, Nancy's cousin went to sleep early and woke up early. Nancy and Paul required someone who was available in the morning, which he was. His drinking did not create a problem in the morning. In addition, he cared about Nancy and her daughter.

Nancy agreed to ask her cousin if he would help and explained that she wanted to be sure his drinking would not interfere. He agreed and said he would be available in the morning. Each morning, Nancy woke her daughter before leaving for work. Her cousin came by thirty minutes later to make sure the daughter was awake and dressed, and then got her to school. The cousin's lifestyle did not change, but he became a reliable support person for Nancy and Paul, though they had initially discounted him.

# Judy

Judy was a grandmother raising her grandson Bobby and a couple of his older brothers. Bobby had been drinking and using drugs with a group of friends. To make matters worse, the older brothers also used drugs at the same locations. The brothers were much older, so Judy turned her focus to "saving" Bobby from the same lifestyle. At Judy's age, it was difficult for her to monitor an adolescent boy who was out partying. We knew she would need help. There was also concern that the older brothers' involvement would make it much more difficult, as they were Bobby's suppliers for marijuana and alcohol.

Our initial focus was to minimize the influence of his brothers. Judy explained to them that she was making an effort to keep Bobby from using drugs, and she did not want drugs or alcohol in the home. Her plan was to carefully watch everyone in the home and to ask the brothers to leave if necessary. Much to our surprise, the brothers agreed that they did not want Bobby to follow the path that had landed them in trouble with the law. They agreed to make it a family project to keep Bobby from using or associating with substance-abusing friends.

The older brothers knew the neighborhood drug users and frequented the locations where such use occurred. If Bobby showed up, the brothers would tell him to leave and report to Judy. In addition, they instructed their acquaintances to stop giving him drugs. Because of their status in the group, people let them know when Bobby was someplace he shouldn't be or with peers who were likely to get him into trouble. The brothers continued to live as they had previously, but their commitment proved invaluable.

The very people Judy had been prepared to evict ended up being key to her success with Bobby. The lesson is to carefully define the help needed and consider all possibilities before striking anyone from the list of potential supports.

A specific request makes it more likely that a person will be willing to assist. Before people are going to help, they will want to know exactly what they are signing up to do. Imagine this scenario: a friend calls and explains that her son is getting into fights, skipping school twice a week, possibly using drugs, and berating her at any suggestion of change. As you listen, you feel heartbroken because she is so concerned about her child and feels worried that he is on a dangerous path. After laying out this overwhelming picture, your friend closes the conversation by asking you to help tackle the behavior. Imagine how your mind would race as you wondered what she expected of you and how you might extricate yourself from this open-ended responsibility.

In contrast, imagine a call where your friend explains that her son engages in some difficult behavior and she is working hard to get it under control. She explains that she is trying to keep him away from a particular group of friends. She is able to call from work to ensure that he is home after school but has no way of telling if his friends are in the house. Your friend asks, knowing you are usually home by three, if you could check periodically to see if there are cars in the driveway or if kids are coming and going. Receiving a specific request is quite different than a friend asking a question that sounds as if she want you to raise her child. In the second scenario, the task is not so nebulous and is easily managed. It fills a large monitoring gap and can make a significant difference in your friend's ability to get her child's behavior under control. Your response to the second call is likely to be quite different from your response to the first.

A detailed request is more manageable, more likely to produce agreement, and generally more effective. An undefined request may result in an attempt to help that has no effect or may actually do more harm than good.

# Brenda

Brenda had been working hard to enforce some new rules in her house, but her son Jason continually responded with intense verbal attacks. Brenda tried to be steadfast but ultimately cracked under the pressure. Brenda's brother, Mike, had a strong relationship with Jason. The two enjoyed activities together, and Jason looked up to Mike. Brenda realized that this relationship might make Mike the ideal person to have present when she attempted to enforce her limits. She explained to Mike that she was trying to set rules, to which Jason had responded aggressively, and asked if Mike would be willing to be present the next time in case Jason responded the same way. Mike agreed, and Brenda called him the next time she planned to enforce consequences. He arrived quickly and was in the room when Brenda explained the consequence to Jason. As expected, Jason became angry and began to yell. Mike quickly intervened and began yelling at Jason about the need to listen to his mother. The two became engaged in their own conflict, which Brenda eventually resolved by convincing Mike to leave the room with her. In the end the intended consequence was never given.

In this scenario, the support person was more than willing to help because he cared for his sister and his nephew. He came over in a sincere desire to be helpful; however, the goals for his involvement were not clear. He agreed to be present to support Brenda in the face of Jason's protests, which is exactly what he did. However, it created additional conflict rather than achieving the desired result.

We then carefully analyzed the conflict and explained the typical pattern to Mike, asking him if he would be willing to try a different approach. Mike agreed that he would ask Jason to take a walk with him if it appeared that a conflict was about to occur. On the walk, Mike would use his leverage with Jason to get him to calm down and express his disappointment and anger over the consequence. Mike would acknowledge Jason's feelings and tell him that Jason's behavior had gotten him into trouble. He would calmly explain that if Jason wanted the freedom he had previously enjoyed, he would need to change his behavior.

Mike's approach to the second fight differed dramatically from the first. He was able to avert the conflict, and Brenda was able to give the consequence. In addition, Mike got Jason to see that he had earned the consequence and should accept it. Mike's involvement made a significant difference in Brenda's ability to be effective.

This case demonstrates the need for clear instructions to those supporting your effort. It also illustrates the need to examine what went well and what did not. This will allow you and your team to create an alternate strategy that may yield a better result. Brenda's process of identifying when a conflict might occur and calling Mike was successful, and Mike responded and came to the house as agreed. But his effort to support Brenda did not help avert the conflict. This told us what not to do at that point. It sent a clear signal that a different strategy must be developed. If we had simply concluded that the effort failed, we might not have asked Mike to return. We would not have built on what had gone well, and we would not have given the family the opportunity to be successful on the next occasion.

# Maintaining the Supportive Relationship

I previously mentioned that you may need some of the people supporting you to remain actively involved in some fashion for an extended time. You are more likely to maintain the supportive relationship if the relationship is not a one-way exchange. In other words, if someone is assisting you, consider ways to reciprocate. If you are receiving help from neighbors to monitor your child after school, it might be a kind gesture to see if there is any way you may be of assistance to that person over the weekend. Could you watch their children on Saturday afternoon so they can run errands? One parent I worked with was an exceptional cook, and she used to bake for a neighbor who had been particularly helpful. She enjoyed baking, and it was a small token of thanks to someone who had played an important role in helping her curtail her son's risky behavior. Another parent had received assistance from a police officer. To express her thanks, this mother wrote a letter to the officer's superior. Police officers' good works often go unnoticed, so the officer particularly appreciated the glowing letter, which was placed in his personnel file at the department.

# Managing Uncertainty

Sometimes you may seek help from someone who has already played a helpful role. He may be unsure if he wants to commit more effort, particularly if previous efforts failed or were unpleasant. This is another scenario in which parents may feel as though the door is closed. If you take the time to educate support people on the scope of your effort and how hard you are trying to curtail the behavior, often they will agree to continue. Another strategy would be to ask what would make this person feel better about providing further help. I have seen cases where a member of the extended family felt frustrated enough by the lack of consequences to consider withdrawing her assistance; she viewed the lack of limits as adding to her challenges in supervising the child. Bu this family member felt much better about providing help after the parent explained the new rules and the plan to enforce them.

Having supportive people involved is crucial to your effort. The job you are undertaking will at times be frustrating, disappointing, and time consuming. It is difficult for parents to manage without the support of other people. This may be unsettling if you do not feel comfortable seeking help from others, but consider whether anyone you know has raised a child without any help from others. And think back to when your child was younger: I am certain there were times when you sought help. This is no different, but the stakes are higher because of your child's behavior, so it is crucial that you seek help when it's needed.

Once you have established a network of support and a plan for how to target your child's behavior, you will have a solid foundation from which to work. You will be able to effectively change some behaviors and target problems that predict challenging behavior.

# Exercise: Plan for Support

1. Identify people in your life who currently provide support or assistance.

2. Identify people you know who might be helpful if asked.

3. Considering what lies ahead, identify specific needs that you will have. (This list will likely be revised as you move through this process.)

4. From your list of people, select those who would most likely be able to fill each need.

5. Plan conversations for each of your needs in which you will explain the situation and make a specific request. You may also include an offer of what you could do in return. The conversation should allow the other person to alter the plan in ways that makes it easier for him or her, as long as it still meets the need.

# Chapter 8

# It's Time for School

Poor school performance and limited involvement in school are major predictors of association with delinquent peers, which directly predicts delinquent behavior. By contrast, school success is predictive of future vocational, social, and economic success. In addition, success in school is typically an important goal that parents set for their children, because of the benefits it confers or simply as a source of pride. It would not be surprising if poor school attendance or poor grades were the challenges that drove you to pick up this book.

Many types of behavior regarding school may attract your concern. You may be concerned about your child skipping school. Some youths attend school but treat it more like a social event than a learning experience. You may also be concerned about your child's responses to people in positions of authority, or problematic social patterns may take place in the school.

# Improve Your Relationship with School

For you to have any influence in these matters, you will need to have a solid working relationship with school personnel and be involved in your child's school activities. Evaluate whether you are sufficiently involved with school. Though logistics may make it difficult, are you involved in the PTA? Do you attend school functions or support athletic programs? Monitoring academics is an important aspect of supporting achievement. To that end, do you check to see if your child has completed homework? Are you aware of upcoming exams? Have you established a time and place for your child to study? Are there rewards or consequences in place for academic performance?

Some parents of youths who have gotten into trouble at school may have an open conflict with school personnel. If this is your situation, the collaborative relationship has clearly been damaged. If you have such a conflict, you need to resolve it immediately. I realize that you may be angry at someone, and in some cases it may be justified; however, being unable to work with people at school will be a direct barrier to promoting the goals you have for your child. I am not saying that you need to spend holidays with the school principal, but you need to be able to work together.

## Identify the Common Goal

An important step toward working effectively with the school staff is to understand, and get them to understand, that you share a common goal. You would like your child to attend school, follow directions, and perform well academically. The school staff want the same thing. They would much prefer to work with a child who cooperates than to argue with your child. You may have disagreed in the past about what should be done to change the behavior; perhaps you blamed each other. Neither approach will accomplish your common goals. It is important that you both start from a framework of having the same goals, then work together to establish feasible strategies for reaching them.

# Who Will Be Involved?

If you have had a turbulent relationship with the school staff in the past, you may need to identify a different person who can serve as your contact. For example, if your conflict has been with the principal, try establishing direct contact with your child's teachers so that you can control your child's behavior and keep the matter from reaching the principal. If the conflict has been with a teacher, you may want to have the principal or some other member of the staff gather information from teachers to minimize your direct contact with this person. You may also ask to have that intermediary attend any meetings if it makes you more comfortable.

# Reach Out

While it may be possible to work around a conflict, it would be more effective to overcome it. This may require a meeting, a phone call, or a letter to the particular staff members involved. The primary message should be that you understand there has been difficulty in the past and that you are concerned, as are they, about your child's behavior. Express your desire to work together to get the behavior under control. If you have reacted angrily in the past, it may be wise to apologize. If they were the ones to get angry, do not be deterred if they do not offer the appropriate apology. The goal is to develop a way of working together. Receiving an apology may make you feel better, but it is not essential.

# Address Scheduling and Communication Challenges

If you choose to schedule a meeting with staff, utilize that time to lay the foundation for working together. Be aware of any protocols for scheduling a meeting or visiting the school. Logistical problems and communication difficulties are frequent sources of problems between home and school. Teachers and other staff members have full schedules with little time for meetings. Given that this may also be true for you, establish some possibilities for times and days that may be better for scheduling future meetings. Also consider which times and days are convenient for them to receive or make calls. Given their full schedules, you may find that some staff members prefer to communicate in writing or via e-mail.

# Address the School's Concerns

Once you have laid the groundwork for effective communication, address any specific concerns you had in the past as well as those the school may have had. It is generally appreciated when parents ask school personnel what they would like to see from the parents or just let them know that their concerns are being taken seriously. In many cases, simply saying that you plan to address the concern will generate goodwill. An acknowledgment or an apology for any lack of response in the past, if that is indeed the case, will let them know you understand their perspective. You may explain that you were overwhelmed at the time and not sure how best to approach your child's behavior at school because you were having similar struggles at home. Teachers and principals are often encouraged when parents thank them for their effort and detail their own plans to address problematic behavior, including the consequences they will give. Such a response lets the school staff know that you are engaged in helping them reach their goal—which is also yours—of changing your child's behavior.

## Request Positive Information

Many parents hear from schools only when there are problems. This frequently makes parents dread answering a call from school or opening an envelope with the school's return address. If you fall into that category, explain that you are fully engaged in addressing the behavioral concerns and would also appreciate the school letting you know when your child is doing well.

## Request Clear Communication and Involvement

If your child has a history of problematic behavior at school, you probably have been involved in meetings about how to approach the behavior. On some occasions, school officials may have used jargon that left you feeling lost and alienated. At the end of the exchange, you may have been handed papers to sign. If this has been your experience, school staff may be happy to hear that you want to be involved and become a force for order in the classroom and that you would appreciate the opportunity to ask questions or seek clarification during the meeting. There are very few school officials who would not honor such a request. In some instances, a carefully crafted request will be a welcome change from the angry or frustrated responses they may have received in the past. In the dynamic outlined above, there is usually no malice present on either side. The school officials may not realize that using jargon makes parents feel excluded. Parents, however, feel alienated when they cannot understand and are forced to sign documents to keep their child in school.

You can imagine how easily this may damage the working relationship. Stating clearly that you want to be included will help overcome or prevent damage to the collaborative effort between home and school.

# "Let Me See Your Report Card"

One obvious area of concern for many parents is their child's grades. When kids begin engaging in troublesome behavior, academic performance typically declines. For some, this is the first indication of trouble. There are many causes for troubles in school, and there are also many strategies a parent can use to address them. In this section, I will discuss some common strategies that can be effective for a child who has the academic ability to perform better in school.

## Are Expectations Appropriate?

If you believe that your child may be in a class that is too advanced or that a learning disorder may be contributing to the difficulty, have your child tested by a trained evaluator to be certain you are not asking for a level of performance that is beyond her capacity, and to determine whether adjustments need to be made in teaching methods. In the discussion that follows, I will address school difficulty only as part of a broader pattern of willful disobedience.

## Know the Homework Assignments

For your child to succeed academically, she will most likely need to complete class work, homework, and exams. To successfully change a behavior, you must monitor whether the desired behavior has been achieved. Thus, to effectively monitor homework, you must first be aware of the exact assignments. This will require frequent contact with the teacher. The severity of your child's academic challenges will dictate how much contact is required, but it should involve as little of the teacher's time as possible. To that end, it's advisable to find out what the teacher's preferred method of communication is.

Sometimes teachers maintain a website that can be checked for assignments. If you do not have access to the Internet, you may need to ask the teacher to print the information and send it home. If this doesn't work, consider how you might gain access to the Internet, perhaps through neighbors or family members. Could you use their computers, or could they check the website and call you with the assignments? If you live near a public library, this may also be a source of Internet access.

Sometimes students have been given a small notebook or an agenda with a class schedule that they carry from class to class. You can also use this to keep track of your child's schoolwork. At the end of each class, your child will write down homework assignments as well as any upcoming exams, and the teacher initials next to the notation that the record is correct and complete. Such a system can also be useful in reporting grades on exams and homework assignments. Of course, the teacher is free to make additional comments if he wishes. When you check the homework, you initial the page to show that it was checked and that the teacher's effort was appreciated.

As with any strategy, it is important to consider potential flaws. If you plan to use a notebook or some form of written communication, it is important that you be able to recognize the teacher's handwriting. Many kids are good forgers. Periodic phone calls or meetings with teachers to check that the system works for them also provide opportunities to ensure that they are in fact signing the document.

Be sure to thank the teachers; we want to also reinforce the desired behavior in them.

Be prepared for the event that child refuses to bring the document home or claims the teacher did not sign it. You have set the expectation that this document must be brought home signed each day. If it is not, you should assume your child did not complete the assignments. You are working to teach your child responsible behavior, and bringing home such a document is a manageable responsibility. If your child had gotten a glowing report from the teacher, do you think he would have forgotten it?

# A Time and Place for Homework

Now that you know the homework assignments, the next step is to ensure that assignments are completed. To that end, it would be helpful to set aside a time for study. Some kids prefer to come home and do homework immediately; others prefer to have a break and do it in the evening. The timing does not matter as long as they complete the assignments.

It is also helpful to dedicate a place in the home for your child to complete assignments. Your child's room could be the chosen place, or you may need to choose another room in the house. During the time allocated for homework, the environment in the study area must support study. Your child should not be watching television; nor should they be on the phone. If the assignment requires computer usage, be sure that homework time is not spent surfing the Internet or on social sites. Some families keep the computer in a common room so it can be monitored; others disconnect the Internet if the assignment does not require access. Some people prefer to study with music playing quietly in the background. However, if the walls are thumping and you hear your child singing, then the stereo may not be a good idea. Go by results on this issue. If your child completes all her homework with music on, great—let her keep listening. If not, then the stereo is not a good idea. Creating an environment conducive to study may also require some changes on your part. If your child studies in a common room, you should not be watching television in that room or adding to the problem in other ways. And checking on progress is certainly acceptable, but otherwise, avoid interrupting the study effort.

## Check Completed Homework

When your child reports that she has completed her homework, do not accept her word without proof. Examine the assignment list and check that each assignment is complete. If she says something like "Don't you trust me?" you may respond: "No, not yet. You're failing in school because you have not been doing your homework." If she has completed her work, reinforce the effort with praise or a favorite snack (alternating between the two) or something else that you both agree on; if she has not, send her back to the study area to complete the assignment.

## Consequences of Not Completing Homework

If communication with teachers reveals a failure to complete each assignment, you should institute a consequence. This same consequence should apply if your child fails to produce the assignment or communication page bearing the teacher's signature. This consequence, or any other, may be used for failing grades on an exam as well. Follow the usual procedure for establishing rules: Let your child know in advance that you see school as important and that you are willing to help when possible, but you expect assignments to be completed and grades to meet a particular standard. When the time comes to provide the consequence, simply explain that school is important and there will be a consequence for not completing assignments or not studying sufficiently to perform well on an exam.

Consequences for poor academic performance are similar to those for any other behavior. You are free to remove access to anything your child is using for enjoyment, particularly anything that may have interfered with school success. Some parents set a length of time to be reserved for study before a child is free to engage in other activities. If your child does not have enough homework to occupy the time, he can go back over the material he missed previously, read ahead, or complete additional work you get from the teacher. Simply explain that school is important, and that his performance indicates that he could benefit from the extra work. As usual, it will be important to plan for your child's response.

## Frequency of School Contact

The frequency of contact and the duration of consequences should fit the scope of the problem. For example, if your child has not done any homework for the past two months, I suggest daily verification of assignment completion from each teacher involved. In such a situation, apply a strong consequence each day, balanced by a strong reinforcement, to get the behavior going. If your child simply misses an assignment once a week, you may not need to check in more than once or twice a week. In this case, consequences and reinforcements may not need to be as severe and may take the form of additional schoolwork or a reward of your child's choosing that is acceptable to you.

# Assess the Need for Additional Work

Many children need tutoring to catch up with the class. Do not assume your child lacks the ability to do the work, however. She may have the ability but choose not to perform. If you suspect this may be the case, ask the teachers for their assessment. Some classes do not build on previous material. For example, a child can perform well on a history exam covering the Industrial Revolution despite having performed poorly on a previous exam about the feudal system. However, in some courses, such as math, current material may build on previous concepts and require remedial work.

## Help from Teachers

If additional work is required, there are various options. If your child's teacher is willing to provide additional assistance, that is a good approach. It is important to recognize that the teacher is going the extra mile to assist your child, and this should be acknowledged in some form. Such appreciation may take the form of a thank-you note or a note to the school principal and school district. You might also have your child assist in classroom chores to show appreciation. As discussed in chapter 7, such recognition will improve the collaborative relationship and make it more likely that the teacher will be willing to help you in the future.

## Help from a Peer

Sometimes the teacher can help find a student who is performing well academically to tutor your child. Where possible, find someone who has enough in common with your child to be able to relate socially. This effort may also address an additional goal if the two develop a friendship beyond tutoring; this could facilitate a social relationship with peers who support appropriate behavior, and help reduce your child's association with the deviant peer group.

The efforts of such a student should also be recognized. I have seen this take many forms. Some people offer money. When this is not possible, I have seen teachers agree to grant the tutoring student extra credit or additional privileges. You may also be able to provide some other compensation. Regardless of the specific agreement, the other student should be included in and agree with the plan. Once your child has caught up with the rest of the class, the tutoring may stop. Should the need arise in the future, this student may be willing to help as a favor to a new friend.

# **Exercise:** Plan How to Work with the School

1. *Determine your expectations for school performance, and state them as described in chapter 3 (homework completed daily, specific time, and so on).*

2. *Identify key teachers and other appropriate members of the school staff and schedule times to meet with them.*

3. *After addressing any problems in the relationship, focus on developing common goals and agree upon a method and required frequency of communication.*

4. *Using communication with the teachers and your own supervision, implement the expectations around school behavior.*

5. *If additional support is required for academic success, be sure this is provided.*

6. *Assess teachers' ability to continue with the plan as designed, and thank them for their cooperation.*

# "Why Weren't You at School Today?"

For many youths, truancy is a primary reason for referral. For others, it contributes to other problems. If your child is getting poor grades, it is unlikely that her grades will improve if she is not in class. For many children, truancy also contributes to substance abuse. Time away from school generally means unmonitored time with kids who are not interested in school success.

## Establish a Daily Routine

You may have discovered that a routine makes it much easier for you to get to work each morning. If your child is up late—whether out with friends, watching television, playing computer games, or surfing the Internet—it becomes less likely with each hour of sleep lost that he will wake up and feel like getting to school. If this contributes to poor school attendance, establishing an evening routine can help address the issue. You can set a time for lights out, or a time when the computer or television must be turned off or when your child must retire to his room.

If your child misses school because he fails to get out of bed, an evening routine will be helpful, but it may not take effect immediately because, similar to jetlag, your child's body has been set to function on the existing schedule. He will be tired for the first few days and will not want to get up and go to school. But for this to work, he must get out of bed. In the case mentioned in chapter 7, Nancy could not be home due to her work schedule, but she was able to have her cousin come over in the morning to make sure her child got up for school. Some families have turned up the volume on the stereo to get a child out of bed. One family left the vacuum cleaner running outside the child's room to get him to wake up. Other families come into the child's room and remove blankets so the bed is no longer comfortable. (I would not suggest this approach if there is any possibility of aggression, however, because it can lead to a confrontation.) One family got the basketball coach to come by the home each morning to drive the child to school. This worked for them because the child liked basketball and did not want to disappoint or anger the coach. In other cases, families didn't directly address waking up for school; they simply explained that it was the child's responsibility to get to school and get there on time, and if he did not, significant restrictions would be put in place. They followed through on this often enough that it became clear to the child that the expectation needed to be met. In those cases, the families offered support in the way of guidance on routines.

## Transportation

Sometimes a child's method of transportation encourages truancy. A complicated mode of transportation or one with gaps in supervision creates an opportunity for detours. In some families I have worked with, children needed to take city buses to school and were required to make connections. Each connection served as an opportunity to find something more entertaining than school. If a child walks to school, his path may take him directly past friends who offer cigarettes or other enticements and encourage him to discontinue the journey to school. In still other cases, youths who walked to school needed to travel through an unsafe area, significantly increasing their dread of going to school each day.

Many such issues can be overcome by providing transportation to school, finding someone to provide transportation, or getting to know those who currently provide it. The most obvious solution is for the parent to provide transportation. Depending on the severity of the truancy, you may need to transport your child to school and walk her into the building, then hand her over to an appointed member of the school staff. If this is not possible, find some form of reliable transportation or someone who would be willing to accept this responsibility. This may be an approved friend of your child's, another parent, a coach, a teacher, or a janitor. The goal is simply to have someone provide reliable transportation.

# Ellen

Ellen attended a school where no transportation was provided by the district. Her parents were not available to drive her in the morning, so she traveled to school via city bus. Her route involved a couple of changes at bus stops, which allowed for multiple distractions as well as boredom. Not surprisingly, many mornings she simply did not make it to school. Ellen's mother was aware that the transportation was contributing to the problem, but she needed to be at work, and they lived too far away for someone else to provide transportation. She also knew that she needed to find a way to close the supervision gaps in the trip to school, so she arranged to go to work late a couple of mornings. She rode the buses with Ellen and introduced herself to the bus drivers, as well as to school personnel who were likely to be available in the morning. She created a plan in which each bus driver would look for Ellen and encourage her to go to school and to have a good day, but would contact Ellen's mother if Ellen was not on the bus. The school personnel agreed to be available to greet Ellen when she arrived and ensure that she attended class. They also agreed to contact her mother if she did not arrive. As a result of this system, her mother knew immediately if Ellen did not attend school and also had an idea of where she might be based on where she went missing. The improved monitoring allowed her mother to either look for Ellen or ask someone to look for her, as well as to provide a consequence the same day.

# Monitoring by the School

Monitoring at school may be helpful in combating truancy. Many schools, particularly high schools, have large student bodies where everyone rushes through the halls during the same four minutes to change classes. This is clearly difficult to monitor and provides an opportunity for children to leave campus in search of other activity. Depending on your child's pattern of skipping school, this may need to be addressed.

Schools have different levels of resources that they can provide, but if your child is slipping out during the gaps in monitoring that naturally occur during the day, you may want to engage the school in closing those gaps. Numerous strategies are available to meet this need. In some cases students were either required to leave class early and arrive at the next class before the time students were generally excused or allowed to travel after the allotted period for changing classes, thus keeping them away from their peers during this time. In other cases, staff members escorted the child from one class to the next; this could be a teacher's aide or someone else with a good relationship with the child. In other cases, an approved classmate was recruited to walk with the child between classes. Regardless of the method, the plan was to ensure that the child was monitored, and parents were immediately notified if the child was not in class. The parents could then locate the child if they had an idea where she might be, or they could plan to impose the agreed consequence that day.

# Involvement in School Activities

Being involved in activities associated with the school increases the likelihood of attendance. As we saw in the case where the basketball coach was involved in the child's morning routine, a child's desire to participate in a particular activity or his relationship with a member of faculty or staff can be useful. Look at the activities, clubs, and sports available at your child's school to see what matches your child's skills and interests. Be careful not to enroll him in an activity in which he is not genuinely skilled if a high level of skill is required, such as athletics, as this could make social relationships more difficult. Whatever the activity, be it drama, music, sports, or computers, being able to participate in an enjoyable activity can create a positive link to school and serve as a reinforcement for attending. If you identify such an activity, contact the supervising faculty member and seek further information on the requirements. Allowances may need to be made, or attendance and grades may limit your child's participation for a time—for example, to a manager for the basketball team rather than a player. Within the program's requirements, take steps to connect your teen to the activity. You may arrange a meeting where the sponsoring faculty member welcomes and encourages him. That staff member may be able to introduce your child to other students in the program and encourage them to welcome him. Such activities and relationships become reinforcing and make it more likely that your child will attend. The adults involved can also serve as supports in your effort to curtail your child's problematic behavior.

## Establish a Relationship with School Personnel for Your Child

Equally important to participation in school activities may be having a relationship with someone on the school staff. Many students have someone at school to whom they can relate. Such relationships should be encouraged and facilitated where possible. This person might greet your child in the morning and regularly encourage her to come to class and perform well in school. In some cases, this staff person may be a resource when she is having a difficult time, or may help with solving problems or defusing potential conflict.

# Denise

Denise had a history of emotional outbursts at school and had several conflicts with her teachers over a couple of years. She began to skip class and eventually stopped going to school. Her parents worked to encourage her to go to school, but she repeatedly found ways to slip out of class or not make it to school in the morning. Denise seemed to have no ties to school and said she felt unwelcome because she had been asked to leave so many times. Her parents had engaged the school in an effort to help Denise return to school and behave appropriately. However, Denise had fallen behind academically and was not eligible for extracurricular activities, so it was a struggle to motivate her to attend. Denise's mother discovered that an assistant principal at the school named Mr. Young was popular with students. Denise's mother asked Mr. Young if he would be willing to get involved. Mr. Young said he knew Denise and would be willing to speak with her and encourage her. The following day, Denise's mother brought her to school and walked her to the building where Mr. Young stood waiting. He greeted her by saying, "Denise, I'm glad to see you here this morning. I know you have Mrs. Johnson's class; I'll walk you there and check on you later to make sure you're having a good day." This may seem trivial, but for a child who felt alienated and unwanted at school, to be greeted by a smiling face made school seem less frightening. Of course there was more work to be done, but this played a major role in getting Denise to return to school.

# Are the Consequences for Truancy Sufficient?

Attending or not attending school should be met with appropriate parental consequences. As with any consequence, the punishment, along with the reward for appropriate behavior, must outweigh the perceived benefit of the inappropriate behavior—in this case, not attending school. In addition, penalties and rewards are not effective if they target a desire that has been satisfied. If your child spends the day doing as she pleases, she may sleep until eleven o'clock, watch television, eat lunch, go to a friend's house where they smoke and play computer games all day, and then return home for dinner. At that point, you give the consequence: no computer access that evening and no going out after dinner. To many teens, that is an acceptable exchange. Your child was able to sleep late, do as she pleased, and avoid doing work or listening to teachers, and she only had to surrender computer access for the evening, after having spent hours on a friend's.

## Making Home Less Pleasurable

So how do we make a consequence effective? There are a couple of options. In some cases, families have devised methods to make children's home life less enjoyable on days when they did not attend school. They may ensure that the child does not have access to television, computers, or favorite foods. Some remove items or disable them before leaving for work. Another effective method is to contact people in suspected hangouts and encourage them to send the child home or to school. Some explained to children that they must complete a long list of chores before using a desired item or privilege that evening. Of course, this must be a privilege where the need has not been met in other ways throughout the day.

# Making Up Missed Work

Other families have effectively used natural consequences. For example, if a child misses school and enjoys the free day, parents might get assignments from teachers, along with some extra work, and have the child make it up in the evening. That way, the child does not get to avoid the work, instead doing it at an inconvenient time. Parents might make their child do the schoolwork on Saturday afternoon, along with a list of chores, so that the child misses out on a day with friends to compensate for the day he missed school. Should you decide to use this natural consequence, you may want to have an additional element in place should your child refuse to do the work. For example, he may be denied use of the car until he has completed the entire workload (assuming that use of the car is still an option).

Feel free to use any consequences and reinforcements you believe will be important to your child. Some rewards may be of such significance that you will not need a lot of planning. You may remember the case of James; his mother's willingness to bring him to school in a robe, slippers, and curlers outweighed any pleasure he had gotten by being late the previous day. The formula will be different for each child, but the goal is to make avoiding school no longer an attractive option.

# **Exercise:** Plan to Improve Attendance

1. *Based on the previous discussion, assess the influences that increase the probability of your child attending school and those that support truancy.*

2. *Using the process outlined in chapter 3 and informed by the identified considerations for school attendance, plan how you might enforce rules for school attendance.*

3. *Develop a method, including frequency of communication with school personnel.*

4. *Devise strategies to address such challenges as daily routine, transportation, and monitoring.*

5. *Develop a strategy to promote and reward involvement with school activities or foster relationships that increase your child's connection with school.*

# Addressing School Behavior

Now that your teen is going to school and doing homework, we can address behavior that gets her into trouble in school. First we need to understand the problematic behavior. Rather than guessing, ask the people involved, particularly those who decide when your child is in trouble. What is it that lands her in trouble? Ask her teachers what she is doing that is problematic, as well as the principal or school counselor, if applicable. Encourage the school staff to be specific about the problem as well as the preferred behavior, so that you are working on the correct issue. For example, if they explain that your teen does not respect class rules, ask them what that behavior looks like. It might mean anything from mumbling under her breath while performing the assigned task to overturning a desk, verbally abusing the teacher, and leaving the room. Clearly the two will require different approaches, and progress will be measured in different terms.

## Add School Targets to Your Behavior Plan

As you may have noticed, I suggested defining the behavior with just as much specificity as you used in your plan at home. There are two reasons for this. It helps ensure you're targeting the correct behavior, and it will also help you make this part of your behavior plan at home. If you provide punishing consequences as well as rewards for appropriate school behavior, you are working much more collaboratively with the school, and this collaboration is likely to generate results. When you support the school's effort to change your child's behavior, you do so exerting more influence than the school will ever exert. For many children, the reason to behave appropriately in school is quite simply that if they don't, their parents will know before they get home, and they will be in trouble. As long as your child performs in school, it is perfectly acceptable that fear of punishment is the main motivator.

## Common Parental Concerns

### Isn't this the school's problem?

No, this is your child's problem, and it happens to occur at school. You may have as a goal for your child to graduate, or not get in trouble, or not be hurt. School challenges will impede your child's chances of reaching these goals. Your child does not seem to care right now, so it is up to you to provide the impetus for him to alter his path. If the school alone was able to change the behavior, it would have done so by now. School personnel do not exert sufficient influence to change the behavior without your support, which is why you must become involved. And if the behavior does not change, the only option the school has is to expel your child, which is certainly not the outcome you desire.

## Rob

Rob was referred to treatment because of school behavior problems and truancy, along with refusal to comply with curfew and problems with substance abuse. His behavior in the school and community had become of such significance that he was on probation at the time.

His parents, Margaret and Phillip, were very concerned and wanted to see him graduate from high school. They established expectations around curfew, approved places in the community, and alcohol use. With the help of their friends and neighbors, they were able to closely monitor Rob's behavior and were consistent in enforcing the established limits. After a couple of months, Rob's behavior had changed dramatically.

However, he was still getting into trouble at school, and his probation officer was becoming increasingly frustrated. Margaret and Phillip felt stuck. They had done what they could to rein in his behavior, but the school was still having difficulty with Rob. While the parents were lamenting that they felt powerless to control Rob's behavior at school, I asked, "How did you get his behavior at home under control?" Margaret and Phillip were clear on how they had changed Rob's behavior. When they finished, I asked, "What would it take for you to be able to do that with his behavior at school?" It was as if a light had gone on, and they felt empowered to change the behavior.

They explained to Rob that school was important and he was expected to attend and participate while following the rules. Next they reached out to the teachers and explained that they were sorry Rob had been disruptive. They expressed their desire to work with the school to get Rob's behavior under control. The teachers welcomed this gesture. The school personnel continued with their efforts, relaying updates to Margaret and Phillip, who thanked them and reported back their response to the behavior in question. Since Margaret and Phillip had been successful in getting Rob's behavior under control at home, and he now knew it was not beneficial to challenge their rules, they were able to change his behavior fairly quickly. Rob was now receiving consequences at school as well as at home when he broke school rules, and he was able to earn rewards in both places for exhibiting appropriate behavior. As you may imagine, this weighed pretty heavily in Rob's evaluation of his behavioral options.

# John

John's parents expressed concern over his school behavior and explained that they expected him to comply with the teacher's expectations. They decided that there would be a consequence if they heard of him disrupting the class. Not long after this warning, John's teacher reported that he had been disruptive. His mother replied that she was not going to tolerate the misbehavior. The next day, his mother took the day off and went to school with John. She asked the teacher if she could sit behind John in class to make sure he did not disrupt class again. Of course, John was uncomfortable with his mother sitting behind him all day in class, but he did not misbehave. John quickly realized that the laughs he may have received for disrupting the class were not worth having his mother sit in on his class. Not everyone has the flexibility in their work schedule to use this strategy, but the lesson is about parents enforcing expectations and their willingness to be involved and be creative in how they accomplish the task.

# Dan

Dan was frequently disruptive in class and was typically called out multiple times in each one-hour class period. Dan's teacher and his mother agreed on a plan where he would earn privileges or consequences in class as well as at home based on his behavior in class. The intensity of the effort had to match the frequency of the behavior. There was little possibility of Dan going an entire hour without one disruption, so they agreed that Dan's teacher would signal him when he had complied with the rules for ten minutes. To avoid embarrassing him, they developed a simple signal: if he met the goal, she would touch his desk as she walked around the room. In the beginning, Dan would receive consequences or rewards based on the number of times the teacher was able to tap his desk. As he began to meet the goals, the standards were raised. First they increased the number of times he had to meet the goal, and then they extended the length of time necessary for recognition. Over time, Dan learned to control his behavior for longer periods, and he was much more manageable in class. This process of increasing the time between rewards is known as "thinning" (introduced in chapter 3), and can be an important part of stabilizing the new behavior.

# Addressing Classroom Outbursts

Addressing outbursts of anger in the classroom may require more planning than that involved in simple disruptions. Based on the severity of the outbursts or your child's ability to manage his emotions, the plan may need to follow the process for avoiding conflicts in the home. Your child should learn to be aware of circumstances where he may become angry and to identify the early warning signs. This will be difficult for him to manage initially, so the teacher should also consider how to identify when an outburst may be on the way. Most teachers appreciate being told of any warning signs that you have observed. Once the teacher knows what to look for, he can warn your child when he senses an oncoming outburst.

There should be a prearranged process for your child, as well as the teacher, to signal the need to leave the class. The agreement should also specify where your child is to go and when to return to class. In some cases, a child might report to a staff member with whom he has a good relationship. In others, the youth may be required to stand outside the door of the class. The child might return to class at a particular time or only when the staff member judges that he is calm enough to return.

If there is an exit plan, a reward should be established for successfully following it. A consequence should be enforced when your child is not successful and has an outburst in class. These rewards and consequences may be the same as those you utilize at home. There is a risk here that your child will learn to manipulate the plan, as we are not only allowing her to leave class but offering a reward for it. To prevent such abuse, we can use strategies like those we used in Rod's case, which follows.

## Rod

Rod was a fifteen-year-old boy with whom we were working to manage his behavior in class. He often became angry and yelled at the teacher. His parents established frequent contact with the teacher to be aware of any difficulty and provide punishment for his outbursts. In addition, Rod was initially rewarded for asking to be excused from the class when he recognized that he was becoming angry. This was supported by the teacher touching her nose when she noticed Rod becoming angry. Rod was also rewarded for asking to be excused after seeing the teacher's signal. When he left class, Rod would go to the school office, where a member of the administrative staff would ask what happened and encourage him to calm himself and prepare to return to the room.

Once Rod had successfully followed the plan a few times, we wanted to ensure that he continued to make progress but also to wean him from the need to leave the room. To this end, we gradually reduced the rewards. At first, we increased the number of successes before he earned a reward. Once he adapted to this, we shifted the plan so that he earned a small reward for leaving class but got a larger reward for staying in his seat and remaining calm. Eventually, the plan changed so that he was still able to leave the room, but only got a reward if he stayed in his seat and remained calm. As his ability to maintain his composure increased, we created a plan where he was rewarded on a weekly basis for avoiding incidents. It is important to note that the reward system was balanced by punishment for outbursts. Eventually, we eliminated the outbursts entirely, and the praise and appreciation he received at school and at home sustained his progress.

## Common Parental Concerns

**My child's teacher really is not nice and may even single her out.**

Your child may have good reason to be angry and frustrated with her teacher, but your child does not have the right to engage in disruptive outbursts as a result. There are many options for managing angry feelings; disrupting class and yelling at the teacher is not a good one. We all come across difficult people, but we manage our feelings despite that dislike. Such skills are learned as a part of growing up. Most youths are capable of learning these skills, which they will need as adults. How well will angry behavior work for your child when she is an adult and does not like her new supervisor at work? Such an outburst is likely to land her in the unemployment line. Many children already have the ability to control their reactions but don't in environments that allow the behavior. For example, would the response to the teacher be the same one given to you? Her grandmother? A group of police officers?

## Peer Influence

Many influences contribute to problematic school behavior. A common contributor is peers who reinforce the behavior by laughing or glorifying the event to other friends. Such an audience works against the teacher's efforts to stop the problematic behavior. Classmates are a continuous presence in school, but there are strategies to minimize their negative effects.

In many cases, youths who get into trouble in class do so with the person seated next to them. It may be that they're actively engaged in disruptive behavior with classmates, or simply acting out with another person's encouragement. If the teacher believes this is the case with your child, you may request a change in the seating arrangement so that your child is seated in the front row or among peers who do not encourage the disruptive behavior.

Often there are many disruptive youths in one class. It is a common strategy for schools to group disruptive children in one class with a teacher trained to manage such behavior. In other cases, it may happen simply because of course requirements and scheduling needs. In any case, the presence of disruptive friends will increase the likelihood of your teen being disruptive. And if your child is in this situation, it may not be effective to request a change of seats. You might need a change of classes, particularly if your child continues to act out despite the teacher's efforts and consistent enforcement of rules at home.

Sometimes you can get classes changed with a simple request made to the school administration, particularly if you are able to enlist the teacher's support. However, if your child was placed in a particular class due to disruptive behavior, you may need to set performance benchmarks with the school before staff will consider a move. Your teen might be allowed to try out a different class for one subject, with further moves based on performance.

Another strategy for addressing peers' tendency to reinforce inappropriate classroom behavior is to introduce new rules for the entire class. In some cases, teachers have implemented class rules that provided consequences to anyone who laughed or cheered for inappropriate behavior. When it comes to more significant outbursts, classmates have been given rewards for not responding and not reinforcing the behavior.

There may be many influences on your child's behavior related to school, similar to those that affect a child's behavior at home or in the community. The primary difference in how they are addressed is the relative importance of each influence. For example, in school, peers are continually present and may have an immediate role in problematic behavior, requiring direct intervention. When your child argues at home, peers' influence may not be as direct, which would warrant a different strategy. The teachers and other school staff have an important role in changing or maintaining children's behavior in school, but parents also have a significant role. Your ability to work with the school is crucial to gaining control of your child's behavior. You must identify the biggest contributors to the behavior and be actively involved in managing the required changes.

# Chapter 9

# "Who Are Your Friends?"

A direct predictor of your child's challenging behavior, along with having exhibited the behavior in the past, is association with friends who participate in and support it. Much of the behavior that caused you to pick up this book involves things children do in the context of group activities. If we do not consider those powerful influences, we are not likely to succeed in changing their behavior.

Many youths who come to the attention of people like me have a history of physical aggression. Much of this fighting occurs in the presence of a group of friends who encourage it from start to finish and cheer during the fight. They may even have created the reason for the fight. In other cases, two groups may get in fights for some reason, or for no apparent reason. Here the role of the friends is unmistakable. When these youths are sent to social programs or counseling, they are frequently taught anger management, but the role of their friends is never addressed. In some cases, kids do not have a clear reason for engaging in the fight and may have never even seen their opponent. Clearly anger plays a minimal role here, at least until the fight actually starts. If the role of the friends is never addressed, what effect will anger management have? Imagine a situation where two groups of five or six teenage boys are facing off on the corner in a heated exchange, and the focus gradually narrows to two potential combatants who are to fight as representatives of their friends. One of the two has just returned from his anger management class. What are his chances of successfully avoiding the conflict by telling the others that he needs to take a time-out and then stepping away to take deep breaths and count to ten? Anger management strategies do not target the main contributor to the behavior—being with these friends in this location without supervision. It would be more effective to aim for his not being there than to expect him to stand up to social pressure by closing his eyes and taking deep breaths.

You need to be an active participant in your child's social life. No, I do not mean that you should be your child's friend and party companion. However, you have a definite role—and a crucial one if there is going to be any behavioral change.

# Assessing Your Child's Friends

Your first goal is to know your child's friends. I do not mean that you should be able to pick them out of a lineup; you need to actually *know* them. You need to know their names and their characters, and preferably those of their parents too. You need to know which friends are closest to your child and likely to have the greatest influence. Then find out more about them. Are they good kids, athletes, drug abusers? Do they get along with other kids at school? Do they even go to school? Are your child's friends known to police in the area? Do they have a record of trouble with the law? Try to find out where they go in their free time and what they do. Inform yourself about the parenting practices of their parents. This will be important when approving places for your child to spend time as well as knowing whom to contact as a resource or for information.

I have given you many questions to ponder, which naturally brings up where to get the information.

## Sources of Information

Don't accept a polite handshake, eye contact, and a smile as sufficient recommendation. Serial killer Ted Bundy was polite and charming; or, for a more benign example, consider *Leave It to Beaver*'s Eddie Haskell. The school staff might be a good source of information.

Your community can be a good source of information. Many communities have a community watch group; most have at least one nosy neighbor. Though the information may not make it to your ears, other people in your community may have observed your child's social relationships. You can also show local police a picture of your child and ask if they recognize her, then find out if they are familiar with her peers. Even if they have no specific knowledge (which is actually a good sign), they may tell you where youths congregate. Go look at these places. Drive by the park and see what's happening; sit across the street from a house and observe the people who come and go. (Please do not do this if there is any reason to suspect that it may pose a safety risk.)

Be involved in as much of your child's life as possible, to understand more about what he does and with whom. If he plays sports, going to a game is a good opportunity to get to know his friends and their parents. If he plays music, the same opportunity exists. Serving as a volunteer at the school or a member of the PTA is another possibility. Work schedules might make this difficult, but I suggest making it a priority.

You can ask your teen about her peers, but be sure to verify the information. Your child may refuse to provide information. I have known parents to follow their teen to see where she went and with whom. This can serve as an information-gathering strategy as well as a consequence for a child's refusal to share information. Other parents explained to their child and his friends that he was not allowed to leave home until his friends had come inside and talked with them. One father wrote a description of the friend's car and the license-plate number and asked people in the community if they recognized it. Many youths communicate today via social networking sites on the Internet. Some parents have gathered information from those sites, in some cases restricting access to the computer until the child had given them access to their friends list. It is common in today's society for youths to have cell phones that are paid for by parents. The details on the monthly bill can be a great resource for information about your child's peers. Call the numbers, particularly those that appear frequently, and find out who answers. If you do not receive the bill, caller ID is another resource.

Parents often feel stymied by their child's refusal to provide information. As demonstrated, you have access to many sources of information to identify your child's social group and gather information for an assessment. Since the peer group is a direct predictor of delinquent behavior, you must know whom your child is with and what they do if you are to create any lasting change in her behavior.

## Keeping Track

Given the amount of information needed to make a thorough assessment and the number of friends children often have, some parents keep notes tracking the assessment process, with cues to remind them of particular information. This may consist of a list of names and contact information for the peers and their parents, with either a check mark or an X to indicate approval or disapproval. You may want to leave space for specific notes, such as times or activities that may be safe or unsafe. Some parents create a separate page for each friend, which allows them to make notes and document sources of information should they need to ask further questions. You may also include a page with contact information for all sources of information that proved helpful. This provides an avenue for verification of information and also helps create a larger network of social supports.

## Exercise: Investigate Peers

1. *Using all possible sources of information, identify your child's friends and where she spends time.*

2. *Begin to assess each friend by gathering information about his or her school attendance, substance abuse, illegal behavior, and positive activities.*

3. *Plan to speak with each friend's parents either by phone or in person to assess the friend and the parents as suitable supervisors or helpers on your quest.*

4. *Observe places your child goes to assess the behavior and activities taking place.*

5. *Determine what peers and places are acceptable, as well as any that may be acceptable under certain conditions, and keep a log of this information.*

# Promote Approved Peers and Activities

If your child has peers of whom you approve, it is important to promote those associations. Create opportunities for those associations and strengthen those bonds. You might ask your child if he would like to invite such peers over to your home or if you could provide transportation to an approved activity. Regardless of the activity, as long as it meets your approval, you should work to promote such a friendship.

Many youths engage in a mix of activities, meaning they participate in some behaviors you support while engaging in others you would question. You must do an outstanding job with your assessment and not simply draw conclusions based on first impressions. Sometimes you may want to promote an association under some conditions but not others, based on your assessment of the activity and the level of supervision. For example, it is appropriate for you to allow your child to associate with a group when they play ball at the community center under the watchful eye of the director but to significantly restrict that freedom after dark on the weekends. Such an approach allows you to diminish the possibility that your child will be in high-risk situations without having to completely extract your child from his social group.

## Monitoring

Peer relationships are an essential focus, and to promote desirable peer activities, we must be aware of where children go and with whom, and what they do once they arrive. Hopefully, you will not always need to provide such a high level of monitoring, but for right now, you need to be aware. I have included a chapter devoted to monitoring (chapter 4), so I will not rehash the nuts and bolts of it here, but I do want to be clear that monitoring and supervision need to be more intense initially than simply knowing where your child may be after school. Potential locations and peers should be assessed and either approved or disapproved. It would also be beneficial for you to know the identity of any adults involved, the level of supervision provided, and the type of activity that occurs.

One effective strategy is to engage your child in activities based on age-appropriate interests or skills he has demonstrated. The more time youths spend in such activities, the less time they have for risky behaviors about which you need to worry. This strategy also engages them in a peer group that's different from the groups associating on the corner.

## Choosing Approved Activities

To successfully promote activities for your teen, it is important to choose activities that involve an expressed interest or skill. If your child has positive activities she once engaged in, it may be worthwhile to promote involvement with that activity once again. Your child may already know some youths involved in the activity, which can make the introduction flow more smoothly.

Many young people are not particularly excited about starting a new activity, particularly one that will minimize their contact with current friends. In these situations, they may be reluctant to offer suggestions. They may also not express any desire to participate. Do not be deterred. You have the ability to give rewards and limit privileges in your arsenal. In such situations, try activity sampling. To do this, create a list of potential activities based on your knowledge of your teen's current or previous interests. Once you have a list, offer an incentive for participating in one of these activities for one week. Provide a reward each day he participates, followed by a larger reward if he participates every day for the entire week. The long-term goal is for him to enjoy the activity enough to want to participate without any incentive.

## Melissa

Melissa's recent behavior had become increasingly concerning for her father, Martin. Melissa had begun failing classes and getting into trouble on weekends. Martin had become particularly worried after she got in a fight, a fairly upsetting incident. Martin was concerned for Melissa's safety and also for her future, especially given her recent involvement with the police. He told me it was disappointing to see Melissa's behavior beginning to damage her future and that she had previously been doing well and participating in sports, particularly as a competitive runner. We agreed that Melissa would be much less likely to engage in fights if she spent more time involved in an approved activity. Martin made an agreement with Melissa that if she returned to the cross-country running program for a week, he would provide her favorite snacks after each day of practice. There was no demand that she continue beyond that week. After the time has passed, Melissa would be free to choose whether to return. Martin was prepared with another activity in case Melissa chose to stop running. The offer was strengthened by a larger reward for participating for the week, as well as stricter limits on her freedom in case she refused. To increase the chances of success, Martin made himself available to provide transportation and told her how happy he was that she was participating again.

After the first day, Martin met Melissa to drive her home and asked how she had enjoyed the practice. Not surprisingly, Melissa expressed disapproval and questioned whether she wanted to continue. Her complaints were so strong that Martin wasn't sure whether he wanted to continue for the week either, or even for the rest of the ride home. Despite his frustration, Martin forced himself to provide the agreed-upon snacks. Over the next week, this scenario repeated itself daily, but the intensity had decreased by the end of the week, presumably because the agreement period was near conclusion.

The following Monday, Martin was preparing to try to engage Melissa in another activity. To his surprise, she showed up to breakfast dressed for running and seeking transportation. Martin was incredulous and wondered what had led to her change of heart. Melissa reluctantly explained that she had met a boy on the men's team. She was interested in him and had been told that the interest might be mutual. In addition, Melissa was a good runner, and the coach had embraced her as a member of the team. Melissa's success, the praise of the coach, her love interest, the praise and support of her parents, and the rewards given by her father (not necessarily in that order) were sufficient to sustain and reinforce her interest in the team, particularly when compared with the restricted freedoms and consequences associated with other choices.

## Cautiously Reinforce Desirable Activities and Peers

As the story of Melissa makes clear, reinforcing participation in desirable activities can pay off for parents. Rewards should be balanced by restricted privileges when children participate in less desirable activities. Given that peer relationships are important to adolescents, the rewards and restrictions need to be particularly meaningful if they are to have an effect. This is no different from enforcing any other limits, but it is an emotional domain for teens, so it is crucial that you resist becoming emotional during enforcement.

Try not to directly criticize your child's friends. This invites argument. A more effective method of expressing your concern is to simply explain, "When you go there with Johnny, you seem to get into trouble; therefore I do not want you to go there with him. If you would like to have him over to watch movies, that would be okay." This approach bypasses debate about the peers themselves, which would assuredly prompt a defensive response, and allows you to effectively limit the association without providing opportunity for debate. You are simply making an observation based on evidence. Your child will likely express displeasure and may attempt to engage you in an argument by saying that you do not like his friends. There is no need to engage in that debate. Simply repeat that under those conditions, he has gotten into trouble, and you do not want to see that happen again because you love him.

# Preparing for a New Activity

Your child's past behavior may make reentry into an activity difficult. For example, a coach may want your assurance that you plan to be involved and that you will be involved if there are any problems. When possible, secure your child's express interest and agreement to participate appropriately. Apologies may also be warranted and necessary depending on the history.

In some instances, other parents may raise concerns. Though this is likely to be offensive and aggravating to you, their concern shows why you want your child to be involved in such an activity.

## Social Skills and Strategies

Sometimes it is helpful to to put your child in touch with another child who's already involved in the activity and can greet him upon arrival, make introductions, or even provide transportation. The coach may be helpful in identifying the most fitting child and making the request. If transportation is offered, it would be a respectful gesture for you to seek the approval of the other child's parents.

To increase the likelihood of success, prepare your child to get along well with others. This may require practicing particular social behaviors or skills. For example, some youths have difficulty joining groups or knowing how to present themselves to participate effectively; practicing the skill will increase the probability of success. The supervising adult may also be actively involved in the introductions or make an effort to group your child with accepting youths. Afterward, you may request the other adults' feedback so you can provide your child with support or advice.

It is common for adolescents not to welcome new participants in their activities. Consequently, it may be important for your child to learn to handle jokes and other barbs without fighting. Based on the level of risk, you may need to ask adults to monitor the situation. This is also a reason to involve your child in activities that match his skills. It is common to force boys to play sports, but if they are not athletic, it may be a recipe for disaster.

In any effort to teach social skills, practice the interaction with your child as it would realistically occur. Following each day of participation, assess how well skills were demonstrated and reinforce appropriate execution or problem-solve around any difficulties. If your child engaged in behavior you are attempting to avoid, such as fighting, the consequence should be enforced.

## Transportation

There are many obstacles to participating in activities. Transportation is a common one. Try to choose activities that do not require extensive travel. However, transportation may be required, particularly if your teen is likely to pass the less desirable peer group along the way. If you cannot provide transportation, you may need to enlist help, possibly from the supervising adult. This approach demonstrates the adult's acceptance of your child's participation, provides transportation, and also provides a natural entrée to the group. In some cases, families have arranged a taxi for a couple of days until transportation could be arranged with one of the participants.

## Finances

Some activities require a financial commitment. For some families, this is not an issue, but for others, it may be a major obstacle. Many families have been given the money by a relative. In others, money is provided in exchange for help with chores. Parents have successfully arranged payment plans for some activities. One of the best solutions to this issue is demonstrated in the case of Lance.

## Lance

Lance was a good basketball player, but he had gotten into trouble in his community and in school and had not maintained passing grades. His misbehavior was increasing in intensity and becoming more dangerous. Lance's mother had begun monitoring his peer associations and enforcing stricter limits. She expressed a desire to have him become involved in sports again in the hope that he would stop associating with the current group. His grades had declined to the point that he was not eligible to play at school, but a recreation center in the area provided basketball. Lance's mother hoped he would be able to play at the community center while improving his grades enough to be eligible to play on the school's team. Upon further investigation, she found that the fee was too high for her. She arranged to meet with the director of the community center. She explained the situation and what she hoped to accomplish and why. The director of the center said he could not allow

Lance to play for free, but Lance could play if he agreed to help coach the younger children. Lance's mother hurried home to explain the agreement to Lance. Lance enjoyed kids and agreed to coach and play at the community center. If Lance's mother had given up when she saw the initial fee, he would not have had the opportunity to play basketball. Her efforts to overcome this challenge resulted in his playing and having the additional activity of coaching, which took away from time he might have spent misbehaving.

# Lack of Activities in the Community

Perhaps the biggest challenge you may encounter in engaging your child in activities is a lack of options in your community. Whether because of funding challenges or geography, some communities lack activities outside of school. In such cases, creativity and effort can yield incredible results. I have seen cases where parents were able to arrange activities by asking people in the area with matching skills if they would be willing to teach and help. Such efforts have resulted in informal clubs focused on the arts, distance running, cooking, music, and academics.

## Larry

Larry was a young teen who began getting into trouble and associating with older peers after school. This peer association had placed him in some worrisome situations with adults and had also begun to put him in the company of heavy drug users. Larry's mother was not available to provide supervision after school and had little support. She decided that an after-school activity would help keep Larry away from his troubling friends. Larry lived in an inner-city community that lacked resources, which made the goal much more difficult. His mother began by considering his interests, hoping to identify resources in the community. Larry had earlier expressed an interest in fixing cars. As you may imagine, a community without funding for a standard park did not have a youth auto-repair club. With some encouragement and a door-to-door effort, however, she found a mechanic who was willing to let Larry come to his garage after school. This was an appropriate activity and location, and the mechanic agreed that he would support the effort with Larry. Each afternoon, Larry went to the garage, and the mechanic ensured that he completed his homework before being allowed to assist. Once Larry had completed his homework, the mechanic taught him skills by explaining his work as he fixed cars. Though he was not an employee of the garage, Larry helped clean up as thanks for the mechanic's effort. There were not many outlets in Larry's community, but by being creative and seeking out resources, his mother found a successful activity.

## Unstructured Activities

Our discussion of youth activities has covered the range from organized school and community activities, to creating community activities, to finding a unique resource. A prosocial activity does not have to be formal. Such activities are certainly nice, but if you live in an area that lacks such opportunity, simply aim for your child to be somewhere with youths who are not getting in trouble and to spend time doing something benign. Playing a video game or watching a movie at one of their homes is preferable to roaming the streets with a peer group that is likely to land your child in trouble. Somewhere in your community there is a child who is not getting into trouble. Find out who that child is and where he goes and begin the effort to have your child in the same place. You may seek this information through people in the community, teachers, police, or anyone you think has the information.

# Employment

Employment can also be a good supervised activity. Larry provides an example where someone in the community was willing to take an interest in him and teach him some skills. However, I have found that many youths have an interest in finding a job. While this certainly seems positive, some precautions must be taken. Not all jobs are created equal in reducing the association with delinquent peers, and thus delinquency. For example, youths working at a nearby fast-food restaurant may take advantage of breaks or trips to take out the garbage as oportunities to exchange or even use drugs. There have been some cases where a child has expressed an interest in working at a particular job, and we later found that the supervisor supported activities we were trying to avoid. I am not suggesting that you not allow your child to work; I am simply suggesting that you do due diligence regarding the job, the supervision, and fellow employees. If you have any concerns, occasionally stop by your child's place of employment or provide transportation to and from work to minimize the opportunity for association with questionable coworkers.

## Handling Money

If your child is using drugs or alcohol, allowing him to earn money may be counterproductive. In such cases, many parents have gotten to know the manager of the establishment and agreed that the parents would be given the paycheck to be deposited in the bank rather than having the child receive the money. The child was then able to request cash from the parents for an agreed use. Sometimes the child protests; he is then simply told that he can choose to receive the money from his parents or he can choose not to have a job.

## Match Your Child's Interests

Ideally, a job opportunity would begin with a specific skill or job interest expressed by the child. For Larry, that skill was fixing cars; for others, it has been construction, hairstyling, or some other skill. If your child has a skill or interest and you know someone who works in that field, that would be an ideal situation for the youth to learn and for you to be involved in monitoring. Barring that scenario, you could take a cue from Larry's story and seek out someone willing to take an interest in a child interested in their work. For some employers, the support of a parent increases their willingness to take a chance on hiring a teen.

Though precautions should be taken when using employment to help reduce your child's association with troublesome peers, this strategy can work very well. An early job opportunity can help youths learn a marketable skill that will serve them later in life. If the use of money is carefully monitored, it provides opportunities for additional prosocial activities. As with any approach, however, you must plan carefully and consider potential pitfalls.

# **Exercise:** Plan a Prosocial Activity

1. *Determine your expectations regarding your child's social activities, and plan how you will monitor and respond to her behavior. Plan how to present this in a conversation with her.*

2. *With your child's involvement, if possible, identify a prosocial activity or a method for trying new activities.*

3. *Assess any obstacles to success and plan to address those concerns.*

4. *Develop a communication method and frequency with a supervising adult that will include information regarding success or challenges faced.*

# Separating from the Group

The previous discussions have covered monitoring, enforcing limits, and finding appropriate activities for your child. As you are undoubtedly aware, there is another factor to be considered. The friends with whom your child currently associates provide a draw that attracts her to them. The specific attraction varies widely, but we know your child finds their company reinforcing in some way. We have talked about ways to counter that influence. Additional steps may need to be taken in some instances to minimize the pull from the identified peers. There are a variety of ways for you to have an influence.

## Joanne

Joanne had begun staying out late and at times did not come home at all. She was not doing well in school and had started drinking and using drugs. Her parents made significant efforts to set limits and promote other activities as a replacement. The concern was that her associates had a substantial influence and were clearly giving her places to stay on evenings when she did not come home. Joanne's parents launched an investigation to find out where she was spending her time, especially questioning her whereabouts on nights when she did not return home. They eventually discovered that there was a man in the area who allowed teens to congregate at his home and supplied them with alcohol and drugs. Joanne's parents approached him and explained that they did not plan to make trouble for him, at least not yet, but pointed out Joanne's age and asked that he not allow her to spend time at his home. This seemed to address the issue for a couple of days, and then the behavior returned. Joanne's parents contacted the police and filed a restraining order against the man. It was explained to him that if he was seen with Joanne, whether at his home or anywhere else, charges would be brought against him. Apparently Joanne's presence was not important enough for him to risk legal charges, and he no longer allowed her in his home. On one occasion, he even made a call to the parents reporting her location.

# Lucinda

Lucinda's son, Terry, had begun getting into trouble and was associating with a peer group that was well known in the community. Lucinda was a strong person and did not intend to allow Terry to continue on his present trajectory. It appeared that all Lucinda needed was a therapist's permission and assistance in focusing her efforts. Once she realized that Terry's presence at the known hangout was indeed a problem, she declared that it would no longer be allowed. Over the next couple of days, if she believed Terry was with the identified group of friends, Lucinda marched to their hangout and dragged Terry home, after explaining to his friends that Terry was no longer allowed to be there and that she was going to come get him if he was. I was not there when she retrieved Terry, but I always pictured her leading him home by his ear. Terry's friends understood that Lucinda would indeed storm their hangout and get Terry, and that she would eventually become angry with them as well. Unwilling to face an angry Lucinda, they told Terry not to return.

There are cases where parents do not feel as empowered as Lucinda, and there are some cases where addressing a child in front of his peers, as Lucinda did, could spark a conflict, even a physical one. Once again, if you believe there is any risk of such an event, do not use this approach. Avoiding this strategy certainly does not leave you without options, however.

# Wayne

Wayne had begun to associate with boys in the neighborhood who were known to be dealing drugs and to be physically aggressive. Eva, Wayne's mother, had recently become aware of this and thought it a likely contributor to his recent behavior. In discussing options, we knew we were going to have to intervene directly, in addition to promoting other activities for Wayne. Eva knew that Wayne was not going to respond well and also knew that his friends would support his efforts to remain with them. Eva was also concerned that approaching Wayne while he was with his friends or approaching the friends was likely to generate intense conflict, which she did not want to initiate. Eva contacted a police officer who typically worked in the area and explained the situation to him. The officer was aware of this particular group and was happy to help reduce their number. Eva and the officer agreed that he would approach the boys periodically and ask if they had seen Wayne. He told them that the police had their eyes on Wayne and were going to keep coming to check for him. As you may imagine, a group of boys selling drugs did not welcome added attention from the police; it was bad for business.

They encouraged Wayne to stop coming to their hangout because he was bringing unwanted police attention. Effectively, they kicked him out of their peer group, which opened the way for Eva to encourage other activities. For Wayne, it allowed him to disassociate without being embarrassed by going straight.

# Scott

After doing some investigation into her son Scott's peer group, Angela learned the names of his peers and their parents' identities as well. She required that Scott provide information about his social plans, including where he planned to go, who would be there, the supervising adult, and contact information. Nonetheless, Scott continued to drink substantial amounts and miss curfew at times. One evening, Angela drove around to the places Scott frequented to see if she could discover where he was finding the freedom to engage in such behavior. Angela found that the mother of one of the teens in the group allowed them to gather at her house and drink, and she also let them spend the night when they had had too much to drink. Angela initially asked the mother to not allow Scott to engage in such behavior because this had contributed to his getting into trouble. The mother agreed but continued to allow the behavior. Angela decided to increase the pressure by telling her that she was contributing to the delinquency of a minor by allowing alcohol use and that by allowing Scott to spend the night without permission, she was also harboring a runaway. Angela expressed her intent to press charges if Scott was found at the house. I imagine that the mother found Angela unreasonable, but she was not willing to challenge her.

The idea of moving to a different area has been pursued by some families. This would successfully remove your child from a particular peer group but would not relieve you of the need to set limits and monitor peer relationships. The conditions at school, in the home, and in your child's behavior that allowed troublesome peer relationships to develop may still be present. In addition, any geographic area has youths who are similar to the ones you just left and are waiting for a new addition to the group. That is not to say that nothing can be gained by moving; it does allow a fresh start and the opportunity to address concerns before friendships become solidified. However, a change of location will not in itself be sufficient to address the issues.

Addressing peer association is complex, but it is of particular importance in the effort to change your child's behavior. There are multiple directions and possible strategies to be considered. It is important for you to examine your situation so as to choose the best path for your family. Make a clear plan for how to address the issue, and also plan for any reactions your effort may incite. As in addressing any behavior, it is important for you to remain consistent, use your supports, and be prepared for the effort.

# Chapter 10

# "What About
My Kid?"

The most effective programs for changing children's behaviors address the systems in a child's life rather than working individually with the child. However, some characteristics may warrant direct attention. Sometimes there may be some work left to do with your child if system changes prove insufficient. You may also encounter a system, such as the school, where cooperation is insufficient and your child initially requires stronger skills.

## Challenges to Address

If you see that your child has challenges related to social skills, anxiety, problem-solving skills, or anything else, you will need to help her develop those skills or overcome those issues. As a parent, you do not have the same limitations in your relationship with your child that a professional encounters, so it is perfectly reasonable that you address any challenges that may make life difficult for your child. However, I would not expect those efforts to have much effect on the challenging behavior until the other issues (for example, peer influence or inconsistent rule enforcement) are addressed.

I am not suggesting that you delay seeking professional treatment for a child who might be suffering from significant anxiety, depression, ADHD, psychiatric needs, or anything warranting clinical attention. However, you should not expect that addressing these issues will alter the troublesome behavior without addressing the other influences.

# Robert

Robert was referred to treatment after getting in trouble at school and at home, but his school behavior was the primary concern. Robert seemed to be a nice, polite child, which certainly did not fit the description provided in the referral report. His father said only that he had difficulty getting Robert to follow directions at times, but the school reported major problems with his behavior. To get a better understanding of the concerns, I had a conversation with school personnel, who cited behaviors such as not remaining seated in class, not doing classwork, and being loud and disruptive. The school allowed me to observe the class so I could better understand the behavior. Upon arrival, I gently opened the door so that I would not disturb the class. It was immediately apparent that Robert was not in his seat, because nobody was in any seat. The entire class was moving around the room doing as they pleased while the teacher sat in helpless frustration making impotent attempts to get the students to return to their seats (assuming they had ever been in them). It seemed to me that being in his seat would have been a safety risk for Robert. I was unsure why the school had selected Robert for referral. Robert's case is a clear example where spending time trying to get him to sit studiously in class was not likely to be effective amid rambunctious peers and a permissive teacher.

# Kevin

Craig and Lauren were distraught over their son Kevin's failing grades and trouble in the neighborhood. He refused to complete homework assignments and seemed to be always in and out of the house and getting into trouble with friends. They were told that Kevin was also not completing his work in class or attending to the lessons. His parents were becoming concerned that Kevin might have ADHD. In our work together, initial efforts were made to establish a solid communication system between the parents and Kevin's teachers. The plan was for the school to notify the parents of academic performance and behavior and for the parents to support the school effort by enforcing established limits. After seeing little progress, we found that Craig and Lauren were not enforcing the limits because they thought that Kevin's behavior could be attributed to ADHD and he needed medication. Though, even with properly treated ADHD, Kevin was unlikely to complete his assignments if nobody was telling him to do so, they decided to take him to a psychiatrist for evaluation. After gathering some background information and behavioral specifics, the psychiatrist explained that he could not distinguish anything in Kevin's behavior that indicated he was not simply taking advantage of his freedom. He further explained that if Kevin did have ADHD, a predictable structure was particularly important even with medication.

Kevin's case provides another example of the need to provide an environment supportive of the desired behavior before work with a child can be effective.

# William

William's parents had a strong working relationship with school personnel. They monitored his behavior and academic progress. He was appropriately rewarded and given punishment for challenging behavior. William had been removed from special classes, placed in mainstream classes, and allowed to join extracurricular activities. In general, William's behavior had been contained, and he was performing much better. There continued to be times when William reacted impulsively when his wishes were not met, and his reaction was disproportionate to the disappointment, including verbal outbursts and knocking over furniture. This behavior took place in the presence of peers who did not support the behavior and wondered why he was reacting so strongly, especially when it was not getting him his way. In a case like William's, where the behavior is being punished, focusing on the child is appropriate and sensible. We provided strategies for him to slow his response and consider his options before reacting. This allowed him time to evaluate solutions and choose one that was more likely to achieve his goal.

Many characteristics may serve as contributors to your child's problematic behavior and need to be addressed. You should leave the more complex issues, such as anxiety, depression, ADHD, and psychiatric disorders, to trained professionals. The skills you have already learned, as well as the following insights, will be of use in developing social skills or at least in supporting the efforts of a trained professional.

# Thought Patterns

Youths who engage in aggressive behavior often assign hostile intent to others and believe other people are out to get them. This perception is the result of attending to hostile cues in the environment at the expense of a broader assessment of the situation (Dodge et al. 1986). This view of the world plays out in various ways throughout the lives of teens. For example, a teacher may raise his voice to call upon a child in a noisy room. A child who views the world through this lens is likely to attend primarily to the raised voice, ignoring the noise in the room, and respond in a way that is disproportionate to the situation. When this lens is applied to interactions with peers, it contributes to increased conflict. A foul in a basketball game or a perceived aggressive look may lead to a fight when taken out of context.

Such thought patterns are most effectively addressed by a trained therapist. However, armed with some information, you may be of assistance. It is unlikely that your child will want to work with you on this problem, but unwanted punishments and desired rewards may offer an incentive. Tell your child you want this to be a collaborative process that will help him earn rewards, and suggest examining previous situations to see if you can help him figure out ways to avoid getting into trouble.

## Identify What Happens

Once your child agrees to engage in the discussion, pick a recent event and ask him to determine at what point it became a conflict. Next ask him to take you backward through the interaction as it developed ("What was happening before that?"). Ask questions about where it occurred, what was said, who was present, what they were doing, what time it was, people's tone of voice, their facial expressions, and so on. The goal is to create a clear image of the scene as it unfolded so you can visualize it as though you were watching a movie.

## Question Your Child's Assessment

Once you have a clear image of the sequence, recapitulate the events from start to finish and ask your child what he was thinking at each step. This question will be new for your child and answering it may take some time and encouragement. If you notice your child assuming the other person was angry or hostile when there were other possibilities, don't get into an argument; discounting your child's perspective will likely end the conversation or create conflict. Instead, just raise the question: "Is it possible that she thought she needed to yell so that you could hear her over the other students in the cafeteria?" "Do you think it's possible that the other boy ran into you because he was going for the ball and didn't know you were going to turn that way?" The goal is to encourage your child to look for other possible explanations for someone else's behavior instead of viewing the world through a hostile lens. If he is able to allow that possibility, the next step is to wonder aloud whether there may have been such possibilities at other times, and if perhaps seeking clarification at such times would have helped him stay out of trouble.

## Track the Thinking

Armed with an open mind, your teen can now begin to challenge his own perceptions. The simple act of attending to his assessment of social situations will allow him to open new possibilities for behavior. Encourage him to track times when he believes someone may be angry with him. He should also note environmental cues that may offer a different explanation for the other person's actions. Finally, have him note his response to the situation. Some find it useful to use a tracking sheet, and some prefer to simply attend to it and report later. While there are infinite possibilities for how to track the process and progress, one option is to use the worksheet I have provided at http://www .DrPatrickMDuffy.com.

## Praise New Evaluations

When your child is able to reevaluate an encounter, make a big deal of it—it is a big step forward. Shower praise on him for taking on the challenge and ask about his process for evaluating the situation. The discussion of his thought process will help define it and make it a more organized and natural part of his method for understanding a situation. When he is not able to reevaluate, provide a consequence if the behavior warrants it, but sit with him and walk through the situation as you did in the initial conversation, offering possible alternatives. Be prepared for the possibility that the other person may have had hostile intent. If so, that requires a completely different direction and another discussion of possible options.

# Manage Emotions

In addition to addressing how teens assess social situations, there is some benefit to broadening a child's ability to understand and manage emotional responses. Aggressive youths often have difficulty accurately labeling emotional states. They may assess difficult emotions like sadness or hurt as anger; because they experience or label other emotions as anger, their responses are more aggressive (Garrison and Stolberg 1983). To help your child understand and experience different emotions, explain that anger is a useful emotion that protects us. Since it serves as a protective measure, anger often covers feelings that leave us vulnerable, such as sadness, fear, or embarrassment.

Carefully dissecting a scenario in which your child felt angry can provide further learning. From the point when she identifies feeling anger, move backward in the chain of events and ask her what thoughts about the situation made her feel angry. Once the thought is labeled, a more accurate emotion can often be identified. For example, someone thinking that "he made me look bad" is probably experiencing embarrassment more than anger. With this new emotional insight, your child can then consider options for addressing the offending party. A teen is much more likely to be able to approach someone to explain that she was embarrassed and suggest how she would like to be addressed in the future if she is operating from a position of sadness rather than anger.

This type of exercise requires many repetitions, balanced by rewarding appropriate and punishing inappropriate behavior. In addition, others in your child's circle should support the effort by prompting her to undertake the emotional exercise if they notice her becoming angry. Catching the sequence early makes success much more likely.

# Generate New Solutions

When presented with social dilemmas, aggressive teens tend to generate a short list of possible solutions (Richard and Dodge 1982). This is partially because they are operating from feelings of anger, but they also typically have poor problem-solving skills. Their list of potential responses may be limited to two: (1) hit him, or (2) look like a punk. If presented with a situation they perceive as hostile and these two options, the chances are fairly high that children will make aggressive behavioral choices. If your child is engaging in aggressive behavior, you can use the same method as above to evaluate his ability to generate behavioral options. Review scenarios to gain an understanding of exactly what transpired. When discussing what preceded the aggressive behavior, ask your child what he saw as possible options. Then see if he can generate a more comprehensive list. In many cases, the responses will be limited.

# Sam

Sam had recently gotten into trouble at school for pushing another child out of the chair at the class computer. When asked about the incident, Sam explained that he completed his work and the other student refused to allow him to use the computer, which was a privilege for those who had completed assignments. When examining the situation, Sam clearly had difficulty developing alternatives. He understood his options to consist primarily of becoming aggressive or accepting that he would not be able to use the computer. To help him brainstorm and evaluate options, we created a table, similar to that in figure 4, that defined the problem and established goals. The table allowed Sam to list possible options and check whether options met his goals.

**Problem:** Sam wants to use the computer, but another student is using it.

**Goal:** To have the opportunity to use the computer and to avoid getting into trouble.

| Options | Get to Use Computer? | Avoid Getting into Trouble? |
|---|---|---|
| Return to seat | No | Yes |
| Push child out of chair | Yes (briefly) | No |
| Yell at child | Possibly | No |
| Ask child to let Sam use computer when finished | Possibly | Yes |
| Ask teacher to allow Sam to use computer after a few minutes | Yes | Yes |

Figure 4

Sam's assessment of the situation, combined with his difficulty generating solutions, limited his ability to create an extensive list of options. The complete list was created through the process of wondering aloud with him, much as the previous section described wondering whether there might be explanations for a person's behavior other than hostility. Once the possible responses were generated, Sam was asked to evaluate whether each approach met the identified goals.

Sam was then asked to use a similar process to evaluate potential solutions to other incidents, including some hypothetical situations that seemed to be within the realm of possibility. It was unlikely that Sam was going to pull out a notebook and create a table for each social dilemma, but the exercise helped him practice and internalize a problem-solving process that would allow him to slow his reactions and evaluate his options. Of course, Sam was not immediately able to manage his reactions; learning a new behavior takes time. Each time he acted out in an aggressive manner, he was given a punishment and walked through the exercise to identify additional options.

When Sam showed an improved ability to problem-solve and generate desirable alternatives, his efforts were reinforced with praise and rewards.

# Seeking Help

To address more complex concerns, such as anxiety disorders, depression, or PTSD symptoms, be sure to seek professional help. I recommend that you seek a therapist who employs a cognitive behavioral perspective (and perhaps consider medication). Cognitive behavioral therapists target specific goals and work in a collaborative manner to make rapid progress. In addition, research supports the use of cognitive behavioral therapy with adolescents to address depression, impulsivity, anxiety, and other common contributors to challenging behaviors (Kendall 2012). Before going to see the counselor, you should have a clear idea of the specific behaviors or struggles you hope to address. It will also be helpful to provide any information you have regarding when and how the behavior is likely to occur.

While some needs are better left to professionals, this does not mean you should stop setting expectations for your child's behavior. In my experience, the reaction of people close to a child is frequently a larger contributor to misbehavior than the anxiety or depression itself. It is very common for adults to stop placing expectations on a child because they feel sorry for him. It is also common to see families attribute all behavior challenges to a diagnosed disorder. Though understandable and natural, these approaches are problematic and work against progress. Even if the therapist is able to completely eradicate the anxiety or depression, you still have a child with no limits and no expectations. I'm sure you understand that this is not conducive to strong results.

# **Exercise:** Work on Problem-Solving Skills

1. Engage your child in a discussion of a recent incident, working backward from the point when the situation became problematic, in order to develop an understanding of the sequence.

2. Your child will most likely leave out his assessments and thinking in detailing the sequence, so work through the sequence again, adding that information, to assess how your child's thinking may contributed to the conflict.

3. Using the strategy defined in this chapter, work with your child to develop the necessary skills or alternative thoughts.

4. Develop a plan to monitor the behavior with adults who are involved.

5. Develop and implement a plan to prompt the new behavior, reward success when it occurs, and assess the challenges when it does not.

# PART 3

# Specific Problems

# Chapter 11

# Substance Abuse

Substance abuse commonly leads parents to seek help for their child. And substance abuse, if not the primary reason for seeking services, is a frequent contributor to troubling behavior. Research into delinquent behavior and substance abuse shows that the same influences that predict a child fighting, staying out too late, or damaging property also predict youth substance abuse (Elliot, Huizinga, and Ageton 1985). If you take a moment to consider this finding, it makes sense. A child in an unsupervised situation with aggressive peers who faces no consequences is fairly likely to be involved in fighting; and it is quite common to find that youths involved in fighting are also using drugs or alcohol. I want to make it clear that not all youths who use substances do so in groups of violent peers. However, they are typically using with substance-abusing peers in an unsupervised or poorly supervised location and with little fear of repercussions.

## Contributors

Since the same elements that predict and support fighting on the weekends also support the use of alcohol and drugs, what sense would it make to address this problem differently? Not much. You may be somewhat disappointed when you read this section and find that there is no magic pill. Substance abuse will be addressed as just another behavior. The same behavioral principles apply, and thus it will be addressed with the same strategic principles.

# Tim

Tim was referred to treatment to address behavior that had landed him in legal trouble. He had been caught stealing and damaging property, and he had not been attending school. His parents were also concerned about a recent increase in substance use. Tim's probation officer was angry about the repeated instances of theft and had made it abundantly clear that any further incidents were going to land him behind bars. Given the gravity of the situation, it was agreed that directly targeting the substance abuse could be placed on hold until the stealing was addressed and the threat of jail diminished. Examination of the stealing offenses clearly demonstrated that the majority were committed on weekends. These offenses occurred outside the scope of Tim's parents' supervision, and each offense occurred in the company of the same two friends. The primary focus was thus reducing Tim's unsupervised time and his contact with the two other boys, particularly when unsupervised. Any violations of the stated rules were quickly addressed with punishment, and rewards were awarded for appropriate behavior. In addition, Tim's parents strongly encouraged him to engage in other activities, which he started reluctantly but then continued. When these changes took effect, there were no more instances of theft or property damage. His parents and probation officer discovered that, as a surprising by-product of their work, the substance abuse disappeared. Though there had been no direct intervention targeting substance abuse, it stopped when his surroundings changed.

# Assess the Use

Attempt to gather information on the specific substances used and the frequency of use. This will allow you to know what signs to look for and how to best detect use. In addition, establishing a baseline of use will allow you to measure progress. Since substance use is typically covert, it may be difficult to gather complete information. If possible, consider utilizing the services of a lab to screen for substances.

# The Role of Medical Facilities

Another benefit of thorough assessment is that you can plan to address any medical concerns related to withdrawal symptoms or continued use. Please be aware that some drugs can have severe withdrawal symptoms that should be monitored in a medical facility. If you are unsure of the dangers associated with a drug, seek medical advice. Please do not mistake my advocacy of a community-based approach as suggesting that appropriate medical intervention or monitoring is unnecessary. Always err on the side of safety.

The National Institute on Drug Abuse has stated that medical detoxification allows physical symptoms of withdrawal to be safely managed. The institute also clearly states that this is a first step and is "rarely sufficient" to stopping use on a long-term basis (National Institute on Drug Abuse 2009, 4).

# Identify the Conditions for Use

Knowledge of the particular substances used is one part of the initial assessment. It is also important to understand the conditions that predict use. For example, are there particular friends whose presence makes use more likely? At what times does your child's use typically occur? Where does she use? For some youths, mood may be relevant and worth noting. Are there any preceding events? Answering these questions can provide information crucial to shaping an environment that does not support use.

A thorough assessment should also include situations or people who make substance use unlikely. Are there places where your child will not use or activities that make use less likely? Steering your child toward these elements and away from those that predict use is an essential part of the approach.

# **Exercise:** Address Substance Abuse

1. *Identify who may have information regarding your child's substance use (your child, other parents, teachers, police), and gather information regarding the substance used, amount, frequency, time, and place.*

2. *Based on your assessment, you may want to have your child tested for specific drugs.*

3. *Consult a professional about medical needs that may arise from stopping the use, and seek care if indicated.*

# Alter the Environment

Once you have assessed problematic situations and protective influences, look into altering your child's environment. This will include monitoring and setting limits on where he goes and with whom he associates, as well as promoting activities that discourage use. If he is using at school or leaving school to use, you may need to focus on increased monitoring by school staff or immediate notification when he leaves school, which results in its own consequence. This effort may necessitate the use of supports.

# Set Expectations

Establish a clear rule to be accompanied by punishments as well as rewards. Drug use is supported not only by the environment but also by the pleasurable effects of the drug, so if your child is to stop, the consequences and rewards offered for undesired and desired behavior combined with the likelihood of being caught must outweigh the perceived benefits of use. Consequently addressing drug use may require significant punishment and reward. Intervention needs to be based on intensity of use. Someone using daily for a year or more is going to require stronger intervention than someone like Tim, who used socially and stopped when he no longer had contact with a certain group of friends.

# Testing

Substance abuse is generally covert; to enforce consistent limits, the behavior must be monitored closely. Some drugs can be detected more easily than others. If your child comes home smelling like alcohol or marijuana—or cologne and breath mints—you may safely conclude he has been using. However, he may be leaving sufficient time between the use and your seeing him to allow noticeable signs to fade, or he may be using a substance that is not easily detected. The most accurate way to monitor use is through drug testing.

There are several ways to approach drug testing. If you have the means, drug tests can be administered at labs available in many communities. Labs can test for a wide variety of substances and do so at different levels. Test kits are also available in many drug stores and pharmacies. In addition, online sites provide a wide variety of test kits for purchase. When seeking a kit, be sure to find one that tests for the drug you are attempting to detect.

# Inform Your Child

Once you have test kits, several considerations should be addressed. First, plan to inform your child of your intent to test. This should follow the same process as explaining rules. Specifically, the plan should be discussed when there is calm in the house. Explain to your child in an unemotional tone that you are concerned and do not want him to be at risk, so you plan to begin random testing, and depending on the results, he may be given a reward or a punishment. Do not expect this news to be greeted with smiles and hugs; he will not like it. Prepare yourself for the response before holding the conversation, and plan to either address his questions or leave the room depending on the response. In severe cases, your child's reaction could be quite explosive; those cases should be addressed with professional guidance. Never put yourself at risk of physical harm.

## Frequency

Another consideration in your plan should be the frequency of testing. Tests need to be administered randomly, yet frequently enough to identify use before the substance leaves the body. Different drugs last for different lengths of time in the body. You should be aware of how long the suspected drug will remain detectable and be sure to test soon enough after possible use or times of high risk. Many stores sell inexpensive breath strips that detect alcohol immediately.

# Plan for Attempts to Beat the Test

To be effective in drug testing, be aware that your teen will likely do anything and everything to undermine the test. A common strategy among users faced with urine testing is to use a urine sample from a nonuser. (If you are testing a teenage boy, it should raise suspicion if the test reveals that he is pregnant, which has happened.) This tactic may be addressed by checking pockets and searching bathroom cabinets before asking for a urine sample. You or your spouse should remain in the room to ensure that the sample is from your child and that your child does not add anything to alter the test results.

Another common strategy is to consume massive quantities of water to dilute the specimen. In one case, the parents woke the youth at 4 a.m. to collect a urine specimen before he could begin such a routine.

The Internet provides a wide range of options for people attempting to disguise drug use. One parent discovered that his child had ordered powdered urine from an Internet site. Another discovered a site that sells attachable false body parts to be filled with a borrowed urine sample.

## Linda

Linda was the caregiver for her grandson and decided to begin testing him for drugs so she could alter his use before too many positive drug screens convinced his probation officer to place him in a detention center. She decided to test randomly but was not thorough in her preparation, and her grandson was able to tamper with the urine sample. Linda was concerned that he would likely be in significant trouble with his probation officer and was indignant over her grandson's attempt to deceive her. The next time, Linda walked with him to the bathroom, stood behind him while he provided the sample, and demanded that he keep one hand on top of his head.

Many concerns can be addressed through a randomization of the process. If samples are requested at random times and your child is required to provide the sample in a different restroom each time, her ability to effectively prepare will be diminished.

One of the most basic strategies is for the child to claim he does not need to use the restroom. If your child tries this, have him sit within sight until he can provide a sample. He may drink something to assist in the process, but do not allow him to leave the room.

Another common approach is to express indignation and refuse to provide a urine sample. If your child refuses, treat it as a positive (dirty) sample and provide the planned consequence. Similarly, if you find that he has made an attempt to alter the test, enforce the consequence. He may also explain a positive result by claiming that he did not smoke but was near people who did; if so, you should enforce the consequence because he either smoked or allowed himself to be in the company of others who were actively using.

# Addressing the Results

Depending on your child's willingness to engage in an open conversation, you can help him consider methods to avoid using. I would not bet heavily on the likelihood of such a conversation, nor would I be concerned if he is not willing to engage in it. Remember, we plan to change the environment around your child in ways that do not support substance use. We do not need him to engage in the effort, though it is a bonus if he does.

It is also possible that your teen may return a negative (clean) urine screen. If your child has a history of drug use and the results are negative, throw a parade. You don't need to actually build floats, but be sure to offer the identified reward and shower him with praise.

## Common Parental Concerns

### Isn't drug testing an invasion of my child's privacy?

Possibly, but the more appropriate question is whether you are justified in doing so to keep your child safe and out of trouble. As a parent, your job is to protect your child, and that may require steps you might not otherwise take. If your child leaves home for a few days, wouldn't you look through her room seeking clues as to where she might have gone? The risk here is high enough to make observing limits to your authority no longer a wise choice. If your child is not engaged in illegal behavior, she should have no objection to being given the opportunity to prove her innocence. Can you imagine the loss of privacy she would face in a juvenile detention center? In cases where youths have stopped using, many have actually looked forward to the next urine screen as an opportunity to show their progress and achieve a goal—and a reward.

# Room Search

Drug testing is one way to address the covert nature of substance use. Another possibly important part of the process involves searching your child's belongings and her room. Simply possessing drugs is illegal, and there is no reason your child should be in possession of a controlled substance unless she has pills you provided with a proper prescription. Like urine screens, room searches should be carefully planned and conducted randomly. You may choose to inform your teen that you plan to conduct searches, but do not tell her when. If there is likely to be significant conflict, you may want to plan your search for a time when she is not home or when a supportive person can be present. You should also plan how you will respond if you do find drugs or alcohol. I recommend providing the same consequence as you would for a positive urine test.

When conducting a room search, you must keep in mind the potentially very small size of a collection of pills or some marijuana, and be sure to check locations that would accommodate something small. The level of intensity of your search should be based on the severity of the behavior. To be completely thorough requires looking for drugs in air-conditioning vents, under mattresses, in backpacks, in pockets, taped to the underside of drawers, in the battery compartments of appliances and games, in pens with the ink removed, and in any other possible location. It is also possible to hide drugs in other parts of the home or the garage. If you suspect this to be the case, keep an eye on your child's movements. One family discovered drugs hidden under the cushions on the family sofa. The older brother was leaving drugs there for the younger sibling to pick up later when sitting on the identified cushion. It is unlikely that you will be able to discover every location capable of holding a small supply of drugs, unless your family pet is a drug-sniffing dog. However, in my experience, most kids are not that creative initially and, when caught, prefer to simply not bring drugs into the home if they know you will be looking.

## Common Parental Concerns

### Isn't a room search a violation of my child's rights?

What right would that be? The right to bring illegal drugs into your home? You have a right to be aware of and control the items brought into your home. You also have a right to protect your child from poor decisions and to change poor behavior. Substance abuse is dangerous enough that it overrides any expectation of privacy your child may have in your home. Would you prefer her to be upset because you searched her belongings, or to be upset because she was on the way to jail or seriously hurt?

# Limit Access to Money

Another helpful step in limiting your child's access to alcohol and drugs is to limit his access to money. Your child may have a friend who is willing to provide drugs or alcohol for free on a couple of occasions, but most users and dealers are unwilling to supply a nonpaying friend or customer for long. In some cases where youths have been employed, as mentioned in chapter 9, parents have controlled the flow of money by arranging to pick up the child's paycheck. They then deposited the check into an account and allowed the child to access money for approved purposes. In cases where youths are not employed, parents have simply refused to provide cash; they provided gift certificates or purchased desired items, but cash was restricted. If you know your child has no legal means of generating cash, you have reason to be suspicious if you find money in his room.

Some parents have not allowed youths suspected of selling drugs to keep money because they knew it was gained illegally, and having money rewarded illegal behavior and reduced their willingness to find legal employment. Such an approach should be carefully considered, however, since confiscating money that belongs to another drug dealer could present safety concerns. In one such case, the father returned the money to the supplier and explained that he had no plans of making life difficult for the drug dealer, but pointed out that the child was on probation and not a "good risk." Once again, this is a potentially dangerous approach.

# Help Your Child Plan a Response

Though you are working to keep your child from people and places that make drug use likely, you may still need to prepare her for being asked why she is no longer associating with the same people or going to the same places, as well as for the possibility that someone may offer her drugs or alcohol. Friends can be persuasive and persistent, and it is unlikely that the conversation will end when a child "just says no." Your child will likely be greeted with attempts to convince her and possibly even embarrass her out of the new behavior. Your child may benefit from help in substantiating the new response. Some youths have been successful by simply saying, "I can't; I'm on probation." Others have said, "Man, I'm getting tested. I can't." If you have had police ask your child's friends about her, she can easily point to that and say, "The police are after me; I can't."

# Common Parental Concerns

## My child has a problem. Will a change in environment really make a difference?

Your child may use drugs or alcohol frequently, but if he were placed in a room with a group of police officers, my bet is that he would survive the allotted time without using. If he were then allowed to associate with substance-using peers, I suspect that he would use pretty quickly. This is obviously an extreme example, but I use it to make the point that youths are likely to be swayed by their surroundings. The goal is to manipulate the environment enough to keep your child from substance use.

## Is my child a "substance user," a "substance abuser," or "dependent?"

You would find as many definitions for such terms as the number of people you ask. Such terms are subjective, though some substances produce physical dependence and require medical attention for detoxification. The definition is not of concern to me. Regardless of what you call it, your child is using and you want her to stop. You may call it one thing and your neighbor or therapist may call it something else. The label does not change the behavior. Whatever you choose to call it, your child is using a substance you would like her to stop using. Beyond the possible need for medical attention, the approach is the same.

## What if there is a genetic predisposition to substance use? Could this still work?

A study conducted at Washington University in St. Louis using two thousand female twins found that substance-using peers strengthened any predisposition toward use (Agrawal et al. 2010). In addition, many people who have a genetic predisposition do not become substance users, suggesting that substance use is not a foregone conclusion even if there is a predisposition, though I know of no treatment options that successfully alter genetic structure. With this in mind, would it not make sense to alter the conditions that make use more likely? Why would we remove a child from those influences, allow her to detoxify in a restricted setting, and then return her to the circumstances that predicted use?

### Isn't substance abuse a disease?

There are many people who support this view, but most proven treatment approaches do not work from this paradigm (National Institute on Drug Abuse 1993). Whether we call it a disease or not, we know that particular elements in the lives of youths predict substance use. Therefore it follows that if we alter those elements, we should be able to alter substance abuse. Such capacity to change behavior has been demonstrated by the approaches in this book. If a person has a cold and enters a room full of doctors, that person will continue to sneeze. By contrast, people with a substance abuse "disease" can typically control it while in the presence of law enforcement personnel if they have a significant aversion to jail cells.

# The Occasional Slip

As a word of caution, be prepared for the possibility that a child who has a clean urine screen or two will then produce a positive drug test. While this is disappointing, do not take it as a failure or a return to the starting point. Your child is learning new behaviors, and a lot of influences can lead him toward substance use. In addition, you and others surrounding your teen are also attempting new behaviors. If you consider all the systems that must work together to support abstinence compared with those that support use, you can understand that slips may occur.

If you have ever gone on a diet, just consider how difficult it is to pass up a piece of cake at a birthday party. There are steps you could take, such as leaving the room before you are handed a piece of cake. You could eat before arriving at the party. You could ask the host not to offer you cake. However, diets are frequently set aside under certain conditions that make eating desserts more likely.

The fact that you ate a piece of cake does not doom your efforts at weight loss, just as an instance of substance use does not mean a lifetime of using. The important point is to move forward with your plan. Provide the consequence in an unemotional tone, as always. It may be helpful to praise your child for previous clean screens and offer to talk about what happened this time. This can open a conversation focused on dissecting the occasion or occasions where the use occurred. Whom was the child with? Where did the use occur? The goal is to understand what led to the use. A secondary goal is to understand how those influences became relevant. For example, was your child in a situation where you wrongly thought supervision was sufficient? Was there a gap in the level of supervision normally present? Once these questions are answered, you can adjust the plans for yourself, your support people, and your child to decrease the likelihood of another occasion of use.

Substance abuse is a problematic behavior that professionals target in many ways. Since the influences that predict or sustain use are the same as those that predict many other troubling behaviors, we are able to change this behavior by using those same strategies. By altering elements of your child's environment, you can create change in ways that will bring substance use under control.

# Chapter 12

# AWOL

Having a child not come home for a night or for several days is justifiably upsetting for parents. Like substance abuse, it puts teens at risk of physical harm and legal trouble. Staying away from home is predicted and supported by elements in a child's environment that allow or facilitate the behavior and should be targeted for change. The principles that apply to other behaviors are also effective in targeting this behavior. This chapter will explain how these principles apply to staying away from home.

## Identify the Pattern

In your initial assessment, attempt to understand any existing patterns. For example, are there particular interactions that take place before your child leaves home, or particular events that may predict the behavior? Depending on the nature of the interaction or event, you may choose to prepare for the attempt to leave home or take steps to decrease the probability of the predictive event.

## Walt

Walt frequently ran away, which was naturally upsetting to his parents. Often he left when confronted with a consequence or limit on his behavior. This was particularly frustrating because it prevented his parents from effectively addressing other challenging behaviors. The pattern did allow his parents to prepare for his departure. Before they enforced a limit with him, they notified several people. They prepared their support people in the area for the probability that they would be called upon to help get Walt to return home. They also informed the adults at the places where Walt was likely to go that he might be on the way and to request that they either call if he arrived or return him to his parents, where he would face an additional consequence for leaving the home without permission.

## Alicia

Alicia also left home regularly without permission. Her mother worked hard to provide for the family and to curtail Alicia's behavior, and she rewarded herself by drinking wine on Friday afternoon. Alicia was angered by her mother's consumption, sparking frequent arguments when Alicia returned from school, which resulted in Alicia leaving home. Alicia's mother was not interested in altering her Friday ritual given the amount of effort she put in during the week, but she understood that this predicted the argument and Alicia's leaving home. They agreed that if Alicia's mother decided to have wine on a Friday afternoon, she would call her mother (Alicia's grandmother) to pick up Alicia from school. Alicia enjoyed spending the evening at her grandparents' house and was able to avoid the confrontation with her mother, and thus did not abscond.

These two cases illustrate how similar principles can be used to keep children from staying away from home. In each case, the parents isolated the sequence that led to the behavior, and they prepared a response and enlisted the help of support people in the area. Walt required a punishment for running away, whereas Alicia did not because the family was able to avoid the sequence. Both cases were troubling to the parents, and both were treated by understanding the influences specific to that child's behavior.

# Where Does He Stay?

If your child is staying out for days without permission, he is clearly being allowed to stay somewhere in the community. You will need to identify the location and the people involved. Chapters 4 and 9 provide strategies for identifying where and with whom your teen is staying. Given the potential safety risks of a child being out overnight with people who support such behavior, you should not hesitate to use some of the more significant strategies outlined in those chapters or to call the police.

Once you have identified the peers or adults who are supporting the behavior, talk with them or have a support person or police officer talk with them. Your goal is to impress on them that staying out overnight is getting your child into trouble and get them to work with you to return her home. Should they choose not to assist you, you can use more forceful approaches, such as restraining orders or police involvement for harboring a runaway. In some cases, the peers or adults involved may prove to be a helpful part of your plan.

## Margaret

Margaret would leave home and stay out overnight whenever she was given a consequence and also on weekends. Her mother asked anyone who might have information about where Margaret was spending time. One of her teachers revealed that Margaret had been spending some evenings with her biological father; the teacher had assumed that this was approved. Margaret and her father had not had a consistent relationship, and he welcomed her visits; he was unaware of how much trouble she had been in and was fairly permissive in his parenting efforts when she visited. Margaret's mother called him and arranged a meeting to discuss Margaret's recent visits. She explained that Margaret had been visiting without telling her and that she had been getting into trouble in school and in the community. Margaret's mother did not initially want to interfere with their relationship, so she requested his support in addressing her behavior. He explained that he had not been aware of the problems and volunteered to assist. They agreed that if Margaret arrived at his house, the father would call the mother to see if she had permission to visit. He would also ask if she was facing any punishment to see if she was attempting to avoid the rules. Depending on the response, her father would return her home, allow her to stay and receive the consequence at his house, or simply allow her to stay if she was in compliance with the rules.

# Bringing Your Child Home

There may be cases where people provide you with information regarding your child's likely location but are not able to return your child home. For example, there may be places where unsupervised youths gather. If you find that such a place is a likely location, you must consider your strategy carefully for the times your child absconds; depending on the situation, there may be a safety risk in retrieving your child. If there is any possibility of a safety risk, do not intervene without the assistance of a trained professional or the police.

If you plan to retrieve your child, prepare by rehearsing when you will go and what you will say. You should also consider whether it would be beneficial to take someone else along—either someone with whom your child shares a strong relationship someone who provides you with support and encouragement, or even a police officer.

When considering the use of a support person, you may also want to consider having that person actually make the attempt to retrieve your teen, particularly if he left following a conflict with you. Whether you choose to make the effort or have someone else do it, you must make clear that running away is not acceptable and will be met with further consequences.

## Addressing the Rules

If your child is leaving in response to punishment, you may be wondering how to give an additional consequence once he has left. The strategies mentioned in chapter 3 about ensuring your child stays home are particularly relevant in this type of scenario. Your child needs to be home to experience the consequence in order for it to be effective. You may also build some incentive into the consequence, such as beginning with a longer period of time that he will be without the desired item or privilege while offering an opportunity to have the time reduced if he accepts the consequence and shows good behavior.

As you can see, the same strategies come into play when targeting your child's absconding behavior as when addressing any other behavior. Tailor them to the situation based on the needs you identified in your initial assessment.

# Chapter 13

# Destruction of Property

Destruction of property is particularly frustrating. Not only does it seem senseless and certain to lead to trouble, but it can be costly in terms of both money and lost items. The good thing is that you already have the necessary information to address this behavior.

## Assessing the Situation

The specific behavior and the type of property destruction will once again determine how you apply the principles outlined in this book. If your child is vandalizing property in the community, you should target this behavior much as you would target behavior like fighting or substance abuse. If children are vandalizing property, there is a strong possibility they are doing so with the support of a peer group and it is certain that they were not under the watchful eye of a responsible adult. Much like Tim's substance abuse, this behavior can often be addressed by simply, though not necessarily easily, filling your child's time with an approved activity and decreasing access to specific friends through punishments and rewards. If your child is not in a setting where the behavior is likely, the probability of it happening drops significantly.

Property destruction commonly occurs in the home during a conflict with parents. In this case, first try to understand how the sequence develops and escalates to the point of property destruction. Develop a clear understanding of the predictors and early warning signs of conflict. Planning to avoid the conflict or redirect it at an early point is an important step in making it less likely that it will escalate to such a level. While the necessary skills and awareness are being developed and practiced, you may want to move particularly valuable items out of reach. While it may seem as if you should not have to do this, your indignation will not replace the vase if it is broken.

# Consequences

If more property destruction occurs, be prepared to meet the behavior with a punishment that fits the offense. Demanding restitution may also be appropriate. This may take various forms. If your child has money, you could require that she pay for the damaged property. She might be required to perform additional chores or services for the owner of the damaged property to work off the cost of the damage. Another possible strategy is for you to take away possessions in compensation for the damaged property.

## Eddie

Eddie's mother had decided she was going to set limits on his behavior and force him to abide by household rules. Eddie frequently became angry in response to her efforts, and his outbursts had previously been effective in getting her to abandon her plans. However, she had become angry and embarrassed by his behavior, which motivated her to be more consistent. When Eddie predictably violated the rules, his mother explained that he would receive the identified consequence. Eddie became angry and started to yell; rather than giving in, his mother left the room. Eddie then increased the intensity of his protest and broke the front door. Once calm was restored, Eddie's mother explained that he would still receive the consequence and that he was also going to be held responsible for the damage to the door. She made several offers to let him fix the door, which were met with responses ranging from agreement to no response to saying he could not fix it. Unwilling to allow him to escape the consequence and restitution, Eddie's mother explained that the door had to be fixed, and she did not have the money nor was she willing to pay to have it fixed. She further explained that she would begin pawning his possessions until she had enough money to have the door fixed, but he could diminish that amount if he wanted to contribute money. Possibly hoping that ignoring her would resolve the issue, Eddie made a few sounds and walked away from the conversation. His mother followed through on her plan to pawn items, beginning with the stereo in his room. Eddie's behavior of damaging property quickly dissipated, and his mother was able to enforce her stated limits.

I hope that you are beginning to notice a trend in how problematic behavior is addressed. The first step is for you to not give any undesired behavior special power, instead viewing it simply as a challenging behavior. Once you are operating from that framework, you can begin to apply the principles discussed throughout this book. Specifically, spend some time thinking about the behavior and the conditions under which it occurs, so as to begin to develop a plan. Formulate a clearly stated rule with accompanying rewards and punishments, and line up supportive people to help in any way needed.

# PART 4

# Putting It All Together

# Chapter 14

# Personalize
# Your Plan

In the introduction, I encouraged you to finish reading this book before attempting to address your child's challenging behaviors. I did this to avoid possible confusion about how to start and what needs to be done first. As you can see, altering a teen's social environment is a large and complex effort. Many elements need to be addressed, and each must be tailored to the needs of your child and family. This is also why I say that reading a book is not equivalent to being enrolled in an evidence-based treatment program with a trained clinician. Many books that offer a new discipline strategy fail to thoroughly address the old behavior. There are multiple contributors to your child's behavior, and if they are not all taken into consideration, you will be left with an insufficient and ineffective approach.

To begin your plan, you must first realize that some things must happen in a particular order. Other things can be accomplished simultaneously. There may also be steps that you are currently unaware of but will find out about as you attempt a strategy.

# Your Willingness and Determination

The first element is your frame of mind and desire to engage in the process. You must view your child's behavior as problematic enough to justify such an effort. If you do not view the behavior as a significant problem, it is unlikely that you will continue for the duration of the effort. Why would you continue if the behavior is not an issue to you? I encourage you to assess this honestly before taking up more of your time with something that is not really an issue for you. I would point out, though, that you read this far into the book for some reason. If the behavior itself is not an issue, perhaps the frequent calls from school or neighbors are an issue for you. Those will continue as long as the behavior continues, and this may be enough motivation to push you through the process.

# Identify Your Role

Secondly, you must see it as your role to address the problematic behavior. If not, you will certainly not endure the challenges inherent in this effort. This work is difficult, and I have not seen many people who were willing to go through such a process if they did not think they "should" be the ones to do so. Let me remind you, however, that if you see the problem as significant, you are uniquely positioned to change it.

# Understand Your Power

Once you identify the behavior as a problem and you agree that you have a role in changing it, you must believe that you, along with others, have the ability to exert an influence. Many parents believe that the troublesome behavior their child exhibits simply happens, because they cannot explain it or understand why their child does it. They may even think that for some reason their child is doing it to them as a personal affront. As an educated reader, you can now understand that certain influences in your child's life predict and sustain your child's behavior. Given that understanding, you should be able to see that altering those influences will change the behavior. Your understanding of the pattern of behavior serves as a road map for changing it.

# Challenge Your Thoughts

Parents may have thought patterns that act as barriers to meeting the necessary conditions. I have attempted to challenge some of those by addressing some common parental concerns. If you currently have such concerns, you may want to revisit some of those responses. If yours are not addressed, I encourage you to examine those thoughts and determine whether they are helpful to you. Please feel free to assess them with someone whose judgment you trust, someone who will not simply agree with you. This is the time for critical analysis.

# Identify and Assess Problem Behaviors

The mind-set just described is essential; this will be a relevant point for anyone attempting to change a child's behavior. Once these conditions are met, there is no absolute direction to take; each child is different, and each set of surroundings is unique. Therefore the next step is for you to carefully identify and assess the behaviors you find troubling. In your assessment, consider events, people, and places, as well as any other influence that seems to increase the likelihood of the behavior. Another factor to consider is the response of the people in your child's life who make it likely that the behavior will occur again. This includes an examination of how you may influence the sequence of events leading up to and following the behavior and whether your response has made the behavior more or less likely or had no influence.

# Start with What You Can Do

I do not blame parents for their children's behavior, but since you are the one with the desire and the power to generate change, I suggest starting with things you can do differently. In addition, you will be the one taking charge and encouraging others to use a particular strategy, so it is crucial that you have a clear idea of what you would like to see done. Parents often need to focus initially on developing new discipline and monitoring practices. As discussed in chapter 3, some families need to focus on attending to the positives and reinforcing appropriate behavior. The majority of cases I have encountered required increased clarity of expectations along with monitoring and enforcement of rules. While factors such as peer relationships may have a more direct influence on your child's behavior, your ability to alter those peer influences will be minimal until you are able to effectively set limits and monitor your child. If your analysis indicates a need, you may choose to include some limits on peers or locations in your initial set of rules, but you must be clear about how you will monitor in order for this to work. For some families, this may not be a challenge; others may need to consider how the child's behavior will be monitored as well as how the child's location and activities will be monitored. You will be unable to address your child's problematic behavior if you are unaware that it occurs or unsure of its context.

# Does a Family Conflict Need to Be Addressed?

In some cases, family arguments are a big predictor of the problematic behavior. If so, carefully include this in your analysis. For example, if you have loud exchanges with your teen over behavior or rules, I would characterize that as a need to develop a different discipline strategy more than as a pattern of family argument. However, if you and your significant other engage in heated exchanges in front of your child, and the child then leaves the home to drink with friends, consider adjusting the manner and timing of your debates. Because your child is leaving home to meet peers in an unsupervised location, those influences also need to be addressed.

# Rules and Supervision Needs

The need for different discipline strategies, increased monitoring, or adjustment of a couple's pattern of arguments may be good places to begin planning. These common needs tend to have a significant impact on children's behavior or are necessary to make other changes, for instance in peer relationships or at school. With that as a starting point, consider whether there may be other needs to be addressed before embarking on this effort. For example, do you and your significant other agree on rules? Do you agree on your roles in monitoring and enforcement? Do you need to develop a strategy for minimizing conflict and removing yourself or someone else from a situation before you can expect to successfully implement the new consequences? Will you need help from others, and do you have a plan for what roles they will play?

# Anticipate Hurdles

I do not want to paralyze your efforts, but I encourage you to visualize how your efforts will proceed and anticipate what may make them challenging or ineffective. In some cases, marital concerns may need to be addressed. In others, couples may be able to work around disagreements. You may also need to consider whether parental substance abuse needs to be addressed or if you are able to use supports to work around any existing use. Some families may be able to simply begin enforcing expectations in the home, while others may need a week to choose the particular behaviors they wish to target or to plan how to avoid succumbing to their child's pressure. No one way is best, because the circumstances you face are unique to you; you should plan accordingly.

# Expect the Unexpected

Once you have created a plan based on careful analysis, be prepared for the possibility that something may still derail your effort. You may cruise through the process, but even the best plan cannot account for all variables. You may attempt to enforce a rule and have your child's grandmother intervene unexpectedly, hindering your effectiveness. If your monitoring plan dictates a daily phone call with the school counselor, your employer may unexpectedly adjust your schedule in a way that conflicts with the call. Do not be deterred by such obstacles. You have the skills and knowledge to address the issue. If part of your plan is not effective, examine the situation carefully to determine exactly what went wrong and how to change it or work around the problem. Perhaps you could wait to enforce a limit until the grandmother is not in the home. Maybe she would be helpful if the effort was better explained, or maybe you need to set some boundaries with her. Do you need to switch communication with the counselor to a written plan instead of a phone conversation, or can you adjust the time of the call or get your work schedule changed? You may quickly see that arguments with your significant other interfere more than expected. You may not have realized that your social life would inhibit your monitoring effort as much as it does. These obstacles do not require you to start over, but you do need to recognize them and plan to address them as you move forward with your plan.

# Assess Plans with All Involved

If your plan involves other people, include them in your assessment. While the phone call with the school counselor may seem like a wonderful plan because you are receiving information, the counselor may be struggling to create the time for the call or having difficulty gathering information from teachers, making it unlikely that this arrangement will last very long. To prevent a disruption in the effort, regularly ask everyone involved if the plan is working for them. They may not have anticipated a conflict or an inconvenience that they find themselves facing. They will appreciate your desire to make it work for them, and you may be able to create a better plan. You may find that you need a different person to fulfill a role. If that's the case, it is better to find out sooner rather than later that your child has been drinking with friends after school, for instance, because your support person was not able to completely fill the role.

# Assess and Plan for Roadblocks

Continuously assess the effectiveness of your efforts by appropriately measuring your child's behavior, whether by the number of days at school, the number of days since the last fight, or participation in an approved activity. On days when you feel discouraged, the measurable progress keep you engaged. If things are not progressing, carefully examine the various systems discussed in this book and identify influences contributing to or allowing the problematic behavior. Apply your new sequencing skills to the behavior or to help identify what broke down in your plan. The other skills presented will serve you in your efforts to adjust your plan, develop a new plan, or seek assistance.

If your plans are progressing well, you may want to check with others to ensure they concur with your assessment and to make a plan for any foreseeable challenges. Begin to develop plans in case some behavior resurfaces or if you identify a new problem.

# You Can Do It!

I told you at the beginning of this book that it would not be easy. I also told you that it would require relentless effort on your part and that of others. However, you are now armed with knowledge of what is effective, so you and your family will be able to create change. Tap into your love for your child and your hope for his future. Remember that you are the most powerful influence on your child. You have the knowledge and the strategies to drive the process of change. Do not be discouraged; be determined. You have the desire, the strength, and the tools to achieve your goals. Stay focused, and look forward to taking warm pride in your child's accomplishments. I've seen families achieve great things following the strategies you just read. You can do it too!

# References

Agrawal, A., S. Balasubramanian, E. Smith, P. Madden, K. Bucholz, A. Heath, and M. Lynskey. 2010. "Peer Substance Involvement Modifies Genetic Influences on Regular Substance Involvement in Young Women." *Addiction* 105, DOI: 10.1111/j.1360-0443.2010.02993.x

Aos, S., M. Miller, and E. Drake. 2006. *Evidence-Based Public Policy Options to Reduce Future Prison Construction, Criminal Justice Costs, and Crime Rates.* Seattle: Washington State Institute for Public Policy.

Aos, S., P. Phipps, R. Barnoski, and R. Lieb. 2001. *The Comparative Costs and Benefits of Programs to Reduce Crime.* Document #01-05-1201. Olympia: Washington State Institute of Public Policy.

Baumrind, D. 1966. "Effects of Authoritative Parental Control on Child Behavior." *Child Development* 37: 887–907.

Blueprints for Violence Prevention. 2006. *Blueprints Fact Sheet: Blueprints Model Program Descriptions.* Boulder: Center for the Study and Prevention of Violence, University of Colorado.

———. 2009. *Blueprints Fact Sheet: Blueprints Promising Program Descriptions.* Boulder: Center for the Study and Prevention of Violence, University of Colorado.

Bronfenbrenner, U. 1979. *The Ecology of Human Development: Experiments by Nature and Design.* Cambridge, MA: Harvard University Press.

Bronfenbrenner, U. 1988. "Foreword." In *Ecological Research with Children and Families: From Concepts to Methodology,* edited by A. R. Pence. New York: Teachers College Press.

Celinska, K., S. Furrer, and C.-C. Cheng. 2013. "An Outcome-Based Evaluation of Functional Family Therapy for Youth with Behavioral Problems." *Journal of Juvenile Justice* 2 (2): 23–36.

Dishion, T. J., J. McCord, and F. Poulin. 1999. "When Interventions Harm: Peer Groups and Behavior Problems." *American Psychologist* 54 (9): 755–64.

Dishion, T. J., K. M. Spracklen, D. W. Andrews, and G. R. Patterson. 1996. "Deviancy Training in Male Adolescent Friendships." *Behavior Therapy* 27 (3): 373–90.

Dodge, K. A., G. S. Pettit, C. L. McClaskey, and M. M. Brown. 1986. "Social Competence in Children." *Monographs of the Society for Research in Child Development* 51 (2).

Elliot, D., D. Huizinga, and S. Ageton. 1985. *Explaining Delinquency and Drug Use*. Beverly Hills, CA: Sage.

Garrison, S. T., and A. L. Stolberg. 1983. "Modification of Anger in Children by Affective Imagery Training." *Journal of Abnormal Child Psychology* 11: 115–30.

Huizinga, D., R. Loeber, and T. P. Thornberry. 1995. *Recent Findings from the Program of Research on the Causes and Correlates of Delinquency*. Washington, DC: Office of Juvenile Justice and Delinquency Prevention.

Kendall, P. C. 2012. *Child and Adolescent Therapy*. 4th ed. New York: Guilford Press.

Miller-Johnson, S., J. D. Coie, A. Maumary-Gremaud, and K. Bierman. 2002. "Peer Rejections and Aggression and Early Starter Models of Conduct Disorder." *Journal of Abnormal Child Psychology* 30: 217–30.

Munger, R. L. 1999. *Rules for Unruly Children: The Parent Discipline Bible*. Daytona Beach, FL: Child Psychology Press.

National Institutes of Health. 2006. "State-of-the-Science Conference Statement: Preventing Violence and Related Health-Risking, Social Behaviors in Adolescents." *Journal of Abnormal Child Psychology* 34: 457–70.

National Institute on Drug Abuse. 1993. *Behavioral Treatments for Drug Abuse and Dependence*. National Institute on Drug Abuse Research

Monograph 137. Rockville, MD: U.S. Department of Health and Human Services.

———. 2008. *Info Facts: Nationwide Trends.* Washington, DC: U.S. Department of Health and Human Services.

———. 2009. *Principles of Drug Addiction and Treatment: A Research-Based Guide.* NIH Publication 09-4180. Rockville, MD: U.S. Department of Health and Human Services.

Office of Juvenile Justice and Delinquency Prevention. 2007. "The Office of Juvenile Justice and Delinquency Prevention's Model Programs Guide." Office of Juvenile Justice and Delinquency Prevention, http://www.ojjdp.gov/mpg/.

Patterson, G. R., B. D. DeBaryshe, and E. Ramsey. 1989. "A Developmental Perspective on Antisocial Behavior." *American Psychologist* 44 (2): 329–35.

Persons, J. B. 1989. *Cognitive Therapy in Practice.* New York: W. W. Norton.

Prinstein, M. J., and K. A. Dodge. 2008. "Current Issues in Peer Influence Research." In *Understanding Peer Influence in Children and Adolescents,* edited by M. J. Prinstein and K. A. Dodge. New York: Guilford Press.

Richard, B. A., and K. A. Dodge. 1982. "Social Maladjustment and Problem-Solving in School Aged Children." *Journal of Consulting and Clinical Psychology* 50: 226–33.

Sexton, T. L. 2010. *Functional Family Therapy in Clinical Practice.* New York: Routledge.

Snyder, Howard N. 2008. "Juvenile Arrests 2006." *Juvenile Justice Bulletin.* Washington, DC: Office of Juvenile Justice and Delinquency Prevention.

U.S. Department of Health and Human Services. 1999. *Mental Health: A Report of the Surgeon General.* Rockville, MD: National Institute of Mental Health.

U.S. Public Health Service. 2001. *Youth Violence: A Report of the Surgeon General.* Washington, DC: U.S. Department of Health and Human Services, National Institutes of Health.

Vaughn, M. G., B. Maynard, C. Salas-Wright, B. E. Perron, and A. Abdon. 2013. "Prevalence and Correlates of Truancy in the United States: Results from a National Sample." *Journal of Adolescence* 36 (4): 767–76.

**Patrick M. Duffy, Jr., PsyD,** is a licensed clinical psychologist who has specialized in working with children and families with significant behavioral challenges since 1993. After working in various programs, including a community mental health center, psychiatric hospital, children's home, and outpatient centers, he began using the evidence-based practice, multisystemic therapy (MST). Through his years of experience, he has served as a therapist, consultant, speaker, and trainer of therapists across seventeen states and in seven countries outside of the United States. Duffy is an annual presenter at multiple conferences that attract an international audience of professionals, and has presented at several conferences across the US and Canada.

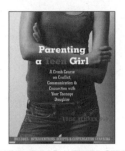